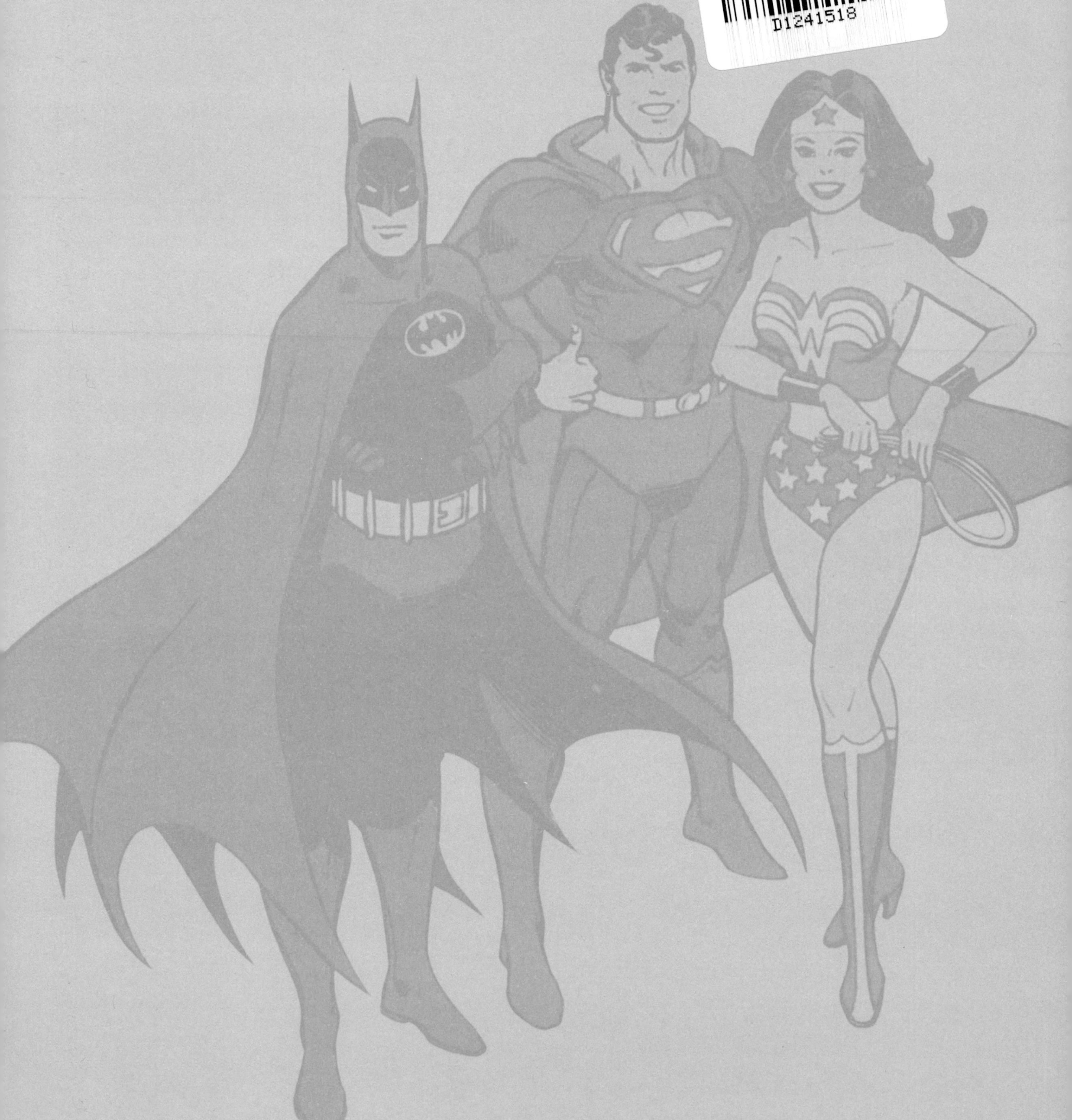

Senior Editor Cefn Ridout
Senior Designer Clive Savage
Picture Researcher Alex Evangeli
Pre-Production Producer Marc Staples
Senior Producer Zara Markland
Managing Editor Sadie Smith
Managing Art Editor Ron Stobbart
Publisher Julie Ferris
Art Director Lisa Lanzarini
Publishing Director Simon Beecroft

Edited for DK by Nick Jones
Designed for DK by Marcus Scudamore at Amazing 15

First American Edition, 2017
Published in the United States by DK Publishing
345 Hudson Street, New York, New York 10014

17 18 19 20 21   10 9 8 7 6 5 4 3 2
007–300031–Oct/2017

Page design copyright ©2017 Dorling Kindersley Limited
DK, a Division of Penguin Random House Company LLC

Published in Great Britain by Dorling Kindersley Limited.
A catalog record for this book is available from the Library of Congress.
ISBN: 978-1-4654-6113-1

DK books are available at special discounts when purchased in bulk for
sales promotions, premiums, fundraising, or educational use.
For details, contact: DK Publishing Special Markets, 345 Hudson Street,
New York, New York 10014 SpecialSales@dk.com

Printed and bound in China by Hung Hing

A WORLD OF IDEAS:
SEE ALL THERE IS TO KNOW
www.dk.com

THE ULTIMATE GUIDE

WRITTEN BY
LANDRY Q. WALKER

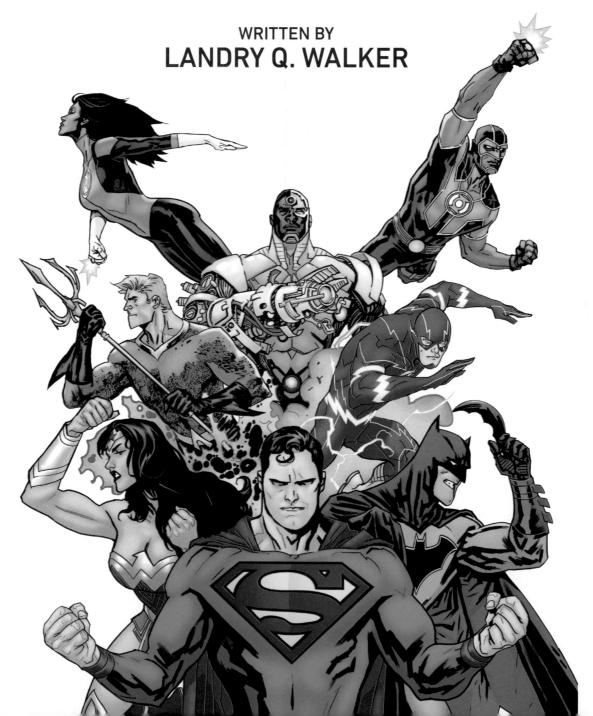

CONTENTS

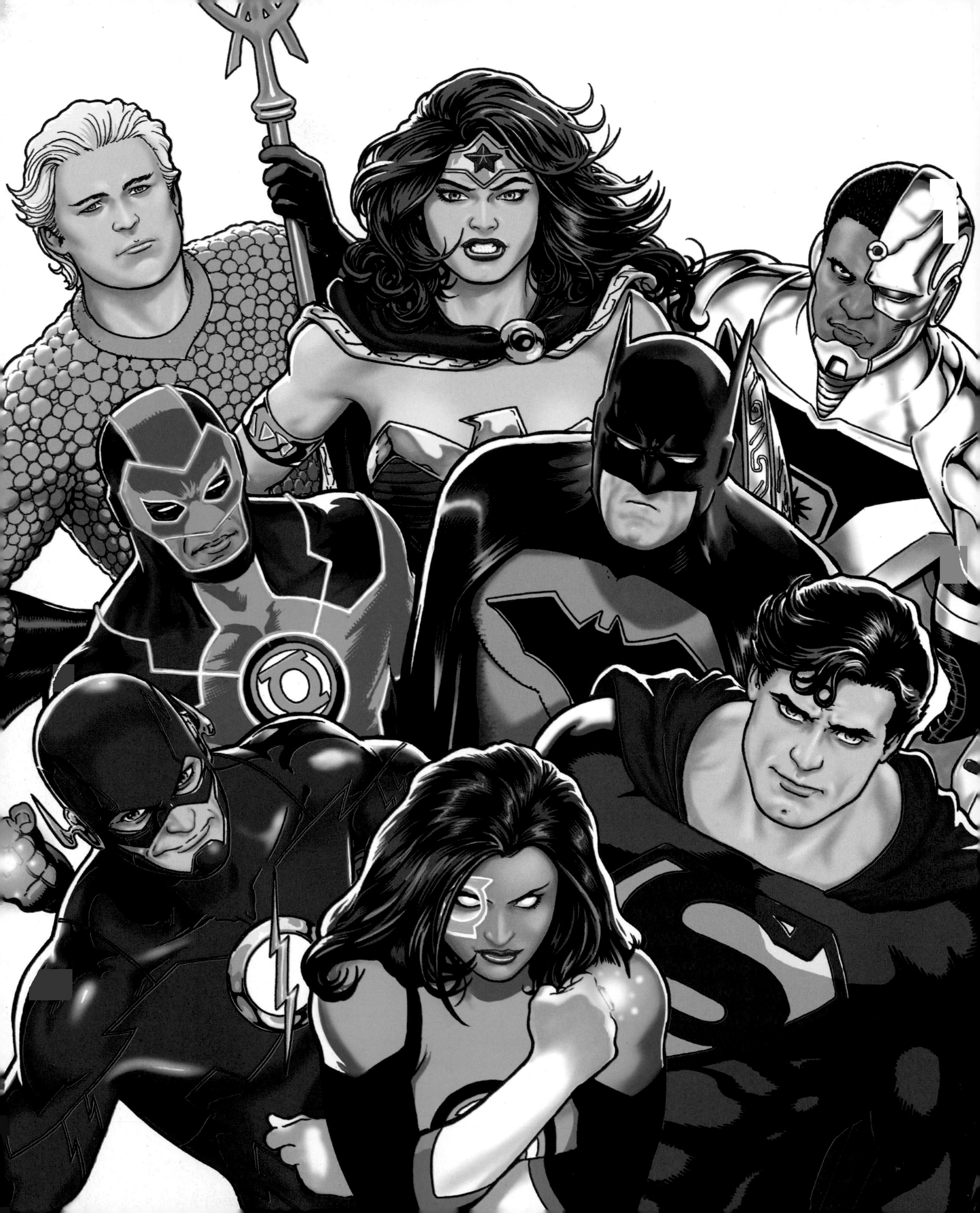

FOREWORD

I can't say for sure who first exposed me to comic books, but I know I was young—maybe five or six—and that I was instantly addicted. In the early 1960s, DC was king of the newsstands and just about every male under the age of 13 worshipped the company's incontestable superstars, Superman and Batman. But the two titles I loved above all others were Green Lantern (will + imagination = manifestation. A perfect recipe for living one's life at any age) and DC's crown jewel, the Justice League of America. All your favorite heroes together in one book? How could anyone resist? I certainly couldn't.

Looking back, those early stories by Gardner Fox and Mike Sekowsky can seem almost primitive, lacking in many elements we've come to identify with modern comics (strong characterization first and foremost: If you just read the dialogue, you couldn't tell Green Arrow from Wonder Woman). But what they may have lacked in sophistication, they made up for in charm, clever plotting and, most important, unbridled imagination. Those early JLA stories opened my young mind to the limitless possibilities of a universe filled with gods and aliens, sorcerers and spaceships, other dimensions and parallel worlds. Just as important, the stories were kid-friendly—something that seems almost shocking given today's hard-edged Super Hero universes. They were written with an innocence and sense of wonder that any child (or open-hearted adult) could easily understand and relate to.

As I grew older, the League grew with me. In the 1970s, a new generation of writers and artists brought a sharper edge, and a more mature palette, to the stories, while always staying true to the book's Fox-Sekowsky roots. I was fortunate enough to enter the world of the Justice League in late 1986 when editor Andy Helfer asked me to wrap up the adventures of the so-called Detroit League. That was supposed to be a one-off gig, but I soon found myself neck-deep in League adventures, working with Andy, co-writer Keith Giffen and an army of artists, led by Kevin Maguire, on a five-year journey through a variety of Justice League International monthlies and mini-series. It was one of the happiest times of my creative life.

In the years since, I've been lucky enough to chronicle multiple incarnations of the League, from the resurrected clones of Justice League 3000 to the monsters and magicians of Justice League Dark and the alternate reality of Justice League: Gods and Monsters. I've also had the pleasure of writing the JL's animated exploits in multiple episodes of Justice League Unlimited and Batman: The Brave and the Bold. I can't help wondering what my League-loving younger self would say if I could travel back in time and tell him that, one day, he'd be crafting the adventures of his favorite heroes. I suspect he'd be amazed, delighted, and profoundly grateful—which is exactly how I feel as I sit here writing this.

Now let's go back to the very beginning and see how it all began…

J.M. DeMatteis
New York
17 April 2017

INTRODUCTION

By the late 1940s, Super Heroes were dead.

It wasn't a super-villain who had killed them, but the shifting tastes of comics fans. In the wake of World War II, reader interest swung away from an initial fervor for these pioneering, superpowered heroes during the late 1930s and early 1940s, towards crime, westerns, science-fiction, and horror comics. Publishers swiftly followed suit, shutting the doors on some of the world's most original, vibrant, and engaging characters.

Soon, what had been a vast multitude of costumed crusaders had been reduced to a handful of die-hard denizens. These hardy few just managed to stay one step ahead of the cancellation axe.

However, in the realm of Super Heroes, death is seldom permanent, and in due course characters were revived, rewritten, redesigned. By the late 1950s, as post-war optimism swept the United States, new, inventive comic book adventures starring costumed crusaders captured the imagination of the public. Chemically generated super-speed; shape-shifting aliens; intergalactic space cops with energy rings; a hero who could shrink by harnessing the power of a star; and a winged man who stayed aloft with help from a rare space metal. Uniting with a few familiar faces, these action superstars changed comic books forever. They banded together as the Justice League—an iconic team that inspired every Super Hero ensemble that followed.

Now, decades later, Super Heroes and their stories have become far greater than the disposable pop-culture entertainments they were originally conceived as. They have become modern myths so deeply seeped into our public consciousness, that it is hard to recall life without them. They fill our movie theaters and are emblazoned on T-shirts, action figures, cereal boxes, and every product imaginable. They're everywhere, and they all have their roots in comic books.

For that we have to thank successive teams of largely unsung storytellers who refused to let these characters fade into obscurity; who saw the chance to do something amazing. They saved Super Heroes, and in doing so made the world a more exciting and richer place. And the dynamic, ever-evolving Justice League is a shining example of their legacy.

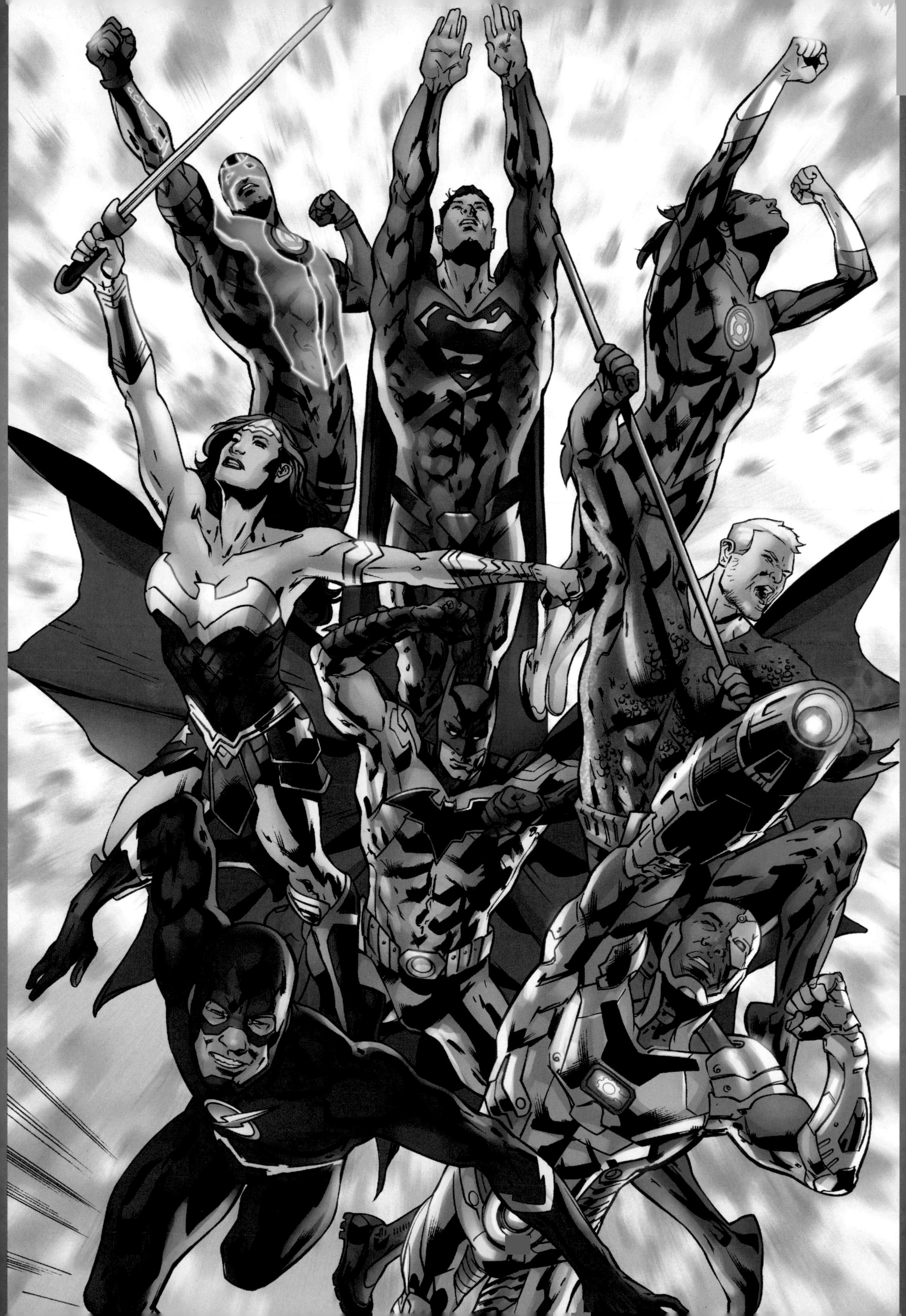

THE WORLD'S GREATEST SUPER HEROES

"United in action, firm in purpose..."

In the 1950s, tastes in comic books had shifted. Tales of atomic rockets, creeping criminals, and macabre horror had become popular, pushing aside the superpowered juggernauts of the previous decade. It was almost the end of a pop-culture era—until the publication of *Showcase* #4 in 1956, which boasted the first appearance of Barry Allen, The Flash. The Silver Age of comics had begun, kick-starting a bold new era of science fiction-inspired Super Heroes. Could a team of such mighty heroes be far away?

Sometimes referred to as the "big seven," Green Lantern (Hal Jordan), Martian Manhunter (J'onn J'onzz), Superman (Clark Kent), Wonder Woman (Diana Prince), Batman (Bruce Wayne), Aquaman (Arthur Curry), and The Flash (Barry Allen) are the mainstays of the Justice League. They occasionally leave the team, but always return.

DEBUT

The Justice League debuted in *The Brave and the Bold* #28 in February/
March 1960. Combining the recently created Martian Manhunter
with the modern reinterpretations of The Flash and Green Lantern—
along with several of DC Comics' most popular superstars—the title
was a huge success. It was easy to see why. Costumed action
heroes merged with modern science fiction in an engaging fusion of
genres. The influence of DC Comics editor Julius Schwartz, whose
background was in science fiction pulp magazines, was evident
from the comic's first cover, which featured a giant starfish from
space. Building upon such fantastic elements, the creative team of
Gardner Fox and Mike Sekowsky took the concept and ran with it,
and soon the Justice League graduated to their own title.

GARDNER FOX

Already a veteran comics creator at the time the Justice
League was conceived, Gardner Fox was a former
lawyer who turned to writing comics during the Great
Depression. He created the first ever Super Hero team,
the Justice League's predecessors the Justice Society,
and introduced the concept of the DC Multiverse.

MIKE SEKOWSKY

Mike Sekowsky entered the world of comics in 1941
when he was 18 years old. Establishing himself quickly,
the artist built a reputation for speed. During the course
of his career he would write, draw, and edit thousands
of comics for a variety of publishers.

JULIUS SCHWARTZ

In 1944, Julius Schwartz applied for a job at National
Publications, otherwise known as DC Comics. Although
his experience with comic books was non-existent when
he joined DC, he had already established a passionate
love of science fiction, having worked with leading
writers Ray Bradbury and H.P. Lovecraft.

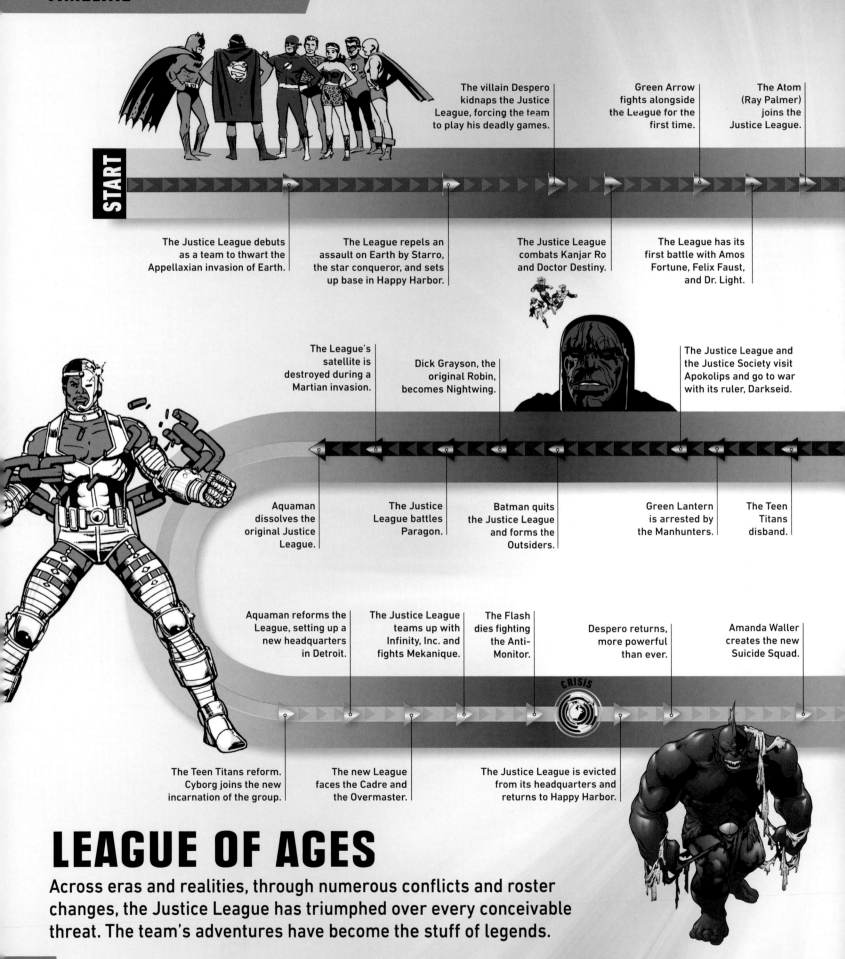

The villain Despero kidnaps the Justice League, forcing the team to play his deadly games.

Green Arrow fights alongside the League for the first time.

The Atom (Ray Palmer) joins the Justice League.

The Justice League debuts as a team to thwart the Appellaxian invasion of Earth.

The League repels an assault on Earth by Starro, the star conqueror, and sets up base in Happy Harbor.

The Justice League combats Kanjar Ro and Doctor Destiny.

The League has its first battle with Amos Fortune, Felix Faust, and Dr. Light.

The League's satellite is destroyed during a Martian invasion.

Dick Grayson, the original Robin, becomes Nightwing.

The Justice League and the Justice Society visit Apokolips and go to war with its ruler, Darkseid.

Aquaman dissolves the original Justice League.

The Justice League battles Paragon.

Batman quits the Justice League and forms the Outsiders.

Green Lantern is arrested by the Manhunters.

The Teen Titans disband.

Aquaman reforms the League, setting up a new headquarters in Detroit.

The Justice League teams up with Infinity, Inc. and fights Mekanique.

The Flash dies fighting the Anti-Monitor.

Despero returns, more powerful than ever.

Amanda Waller creates the new Suicide Squad.

CRISIS

The Teen Titans reform. Cyborg joins the new incarnation of the group.

The new League faces the Cadre and the Overmaster.

The Justice League is evicted from its headquarters and returns to Happy Harbor.

LEAGUE OF AGES

Across eras and realities, through numerous conflicts and roster changes, the Justice League has triumphed over every conceivable threat. The team's adventures have become the stuff of legends.

Batman and Owlman face-off when the Crime Syndicate attacks the Justice League and the Justice Society.

The Teen Titans take on Mister Twister in their debut adventure.

Having formed the Royal Flush Gang, Amos Fortune returns to battle the League.

The Justice League has its first team-up with the Justice Society.

Hawkman joins the League.

The Justice League encounters the psychoactive villain called the Key.

The Justice League visits Earth-S.

The League faces Eclipso in the first of many run-ins with the villain.

The League meets the Champions of Angor.

Zatanna searches for her missing father with help from the League.

The Justice League combats Nazis on Earth-X.

The League encounters the Seven Soldiers of Victory and fights Nebula Man.

League 'mascot' Snapper Carr betrays his friends to The Joker. The League creates a new satellite base.

Glorious Godfrey attempts to turn humanity against the League.

Wally West retires as Kid Flash and becomes the second Flash.

A new League forms in the old Happy Harbor headquarters.

The Justice League battles the Gray Man and the Cell.

Rocket Red 7 is revealed to be a Manhunter agent. Rocket Red 4 joins the League.

Vibe and Steel are killed, leading to the break up of the Justice League of Detroit.

The Champions of Angor attempt to rid the world of nuclear missiles.

Maxwell Lord arranges for the League to gain International status.

Timeline key

▶ The Early Years   ▶ Down to Earth   ▶ Heroes Reborn   ▶ A World Reborn

▶ Cosmic Defenders   ▶ International Expansion   ▶ Heroes Fall   ◉ Cosmic shifts

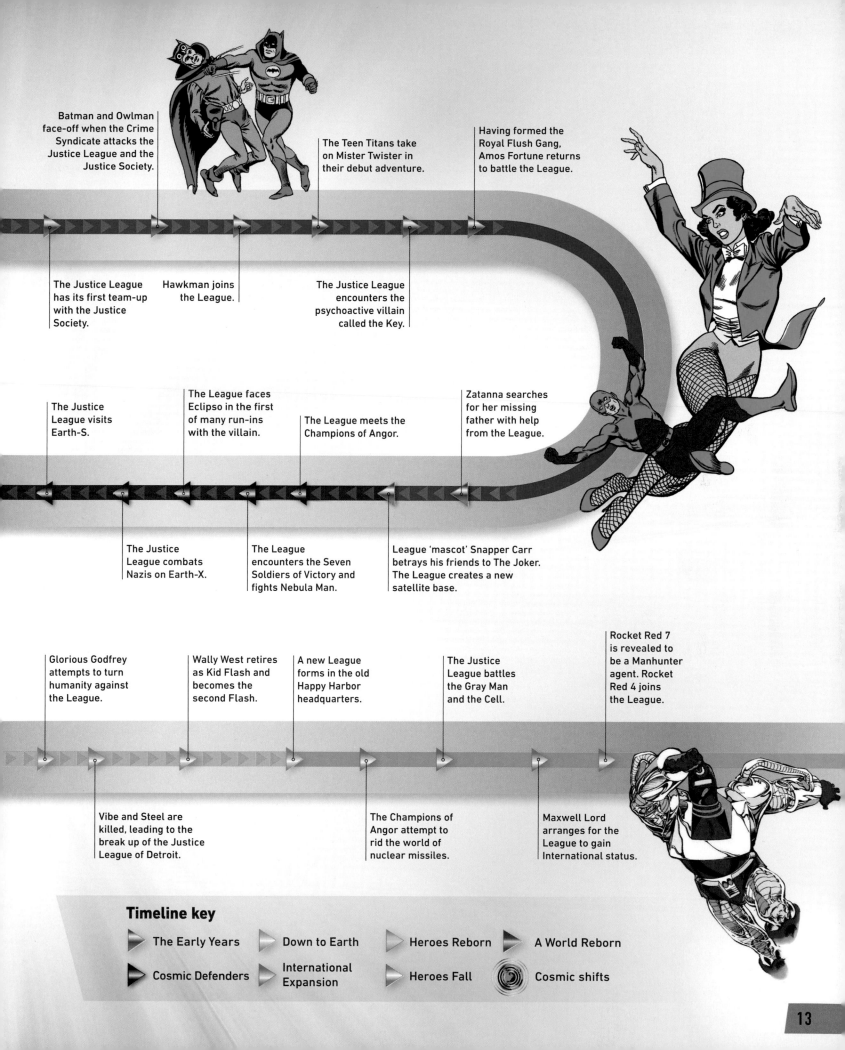

The League faces Major Disaster and the Injustice League.

Justice League Antarctica is formed, and almost immediately disbands!

Two new teams spin out of the Justice League—Extreme Justice and Justice League Task Force.

The Justice League meets Manga Khan and L-Ron.

The European branch of the Justice League opens in Paris.

The Scarlet Skier and Mr. Nebula arrive on Earth.

The Extremists from Angor attack.

Two former Champions of Angor—Silver Sorceress and Blue Jay—join Justice League Europe.

All versions of the Justice League are disbanded.

The Flash has proved pivotal to the history of the League. Killed in the first Crisis, Barry Allen returns to life during the Final Crisis, and triggers the reality-altering Flashpoint.

In the absence of other leadership, Doctor Light takes over as team leader.

Barry Allen is reborn, returning as The Flash.

Nekron launches his assault with his undead Black Lanterns.

Darkseid sends Batman into the past. Dick Grayson retires as Nightwing to become the new Batman.

Libra attacks the League, heralding Darkseid's attempt at rebirth. The Martian Manhunter dies.

Lex Luthor forms a deadly new Injustice League with all-new members.

Barry Allen runs backward in time to save his mother. Flashpoint occurs.

David Graves attacks the Justice League.

FLASHPOINT

Red Arrow is critically injured by Prometheus, who is executed by Green Arrow.

Cyborg, Donna Troy, and Mon-El join the Justice League. Dick Grayson, as Batman, becomes team leader.

In a new reality, the Justice League forms for the first time. The team battles Darkseid.

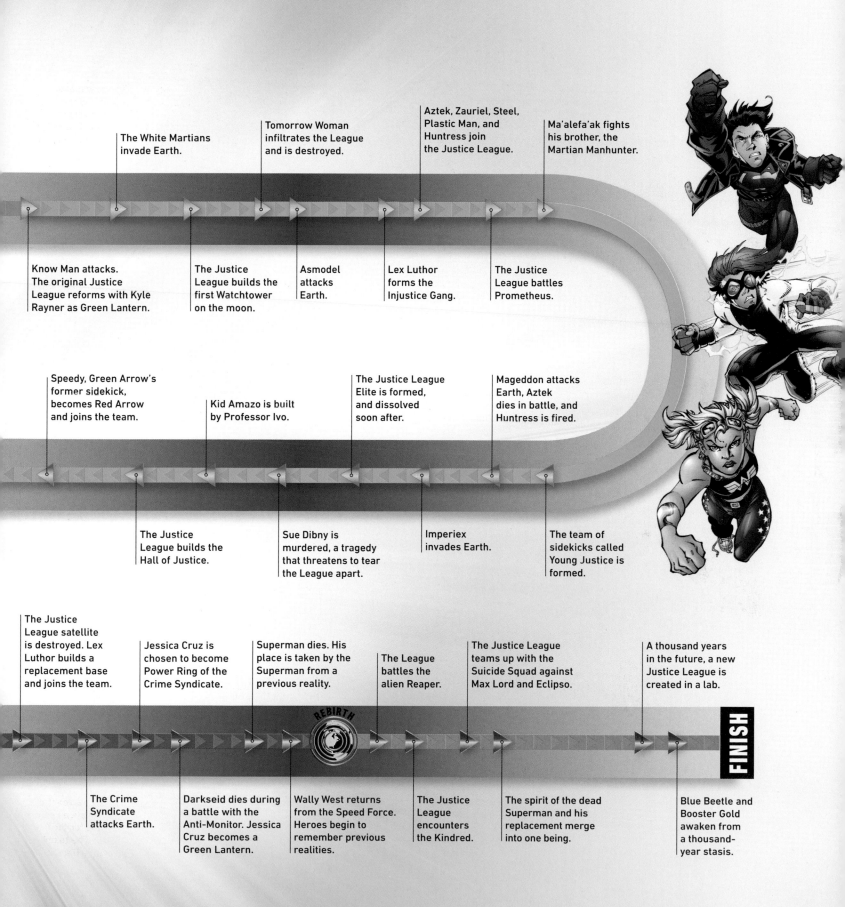

The White Martians invade Earth.

Tomorrow Woman infiltrates the League and is destroyed.

Aztek, Zauriel, Steel, Plastic Man, and Huntress join the Justice League.

Ma'alefa'ak fights his brother, the Martian Manhunter.

Know Man attacks. The original Justice League reforms with Kyle Rayner as Green Lantern.

The Justice League builds the first Watchtower on the moon.

Asmodel attacks Earth.

Lex Luthor forms the Injustice Gang.

The Justice League battles Prometheus.

Speedy, Green Arrow's former sidekick, becomes Red Arrow and joins the team.

Kid Amazo is built by Professor Ivo.

The Justice League Elite is formed, and dissolved soon after.

Mageddon attacks Earth, Aztek dies in battle, and Huntress is fired.

The Justice League builds the Hall of Justice.

Sue Dibny is murdered, a tragedy that threatens to tear the League apart.

Imperiex invades Earth.

The team of sidekicks called Young Justice is formed.

The Justice League satellite is destroyed. Lex Luthor builds a replacement base and joins the team.

Jessica Cruz is chosen to become Power Ring of the Crime Syndicate.

Superman dies. His place is taken by the Superman from a previous reality.

The League battles the alien Reaper.

The Justice League teams up with the Suicide Squad against Max Lord and Eclipso.

A thousand years in the future, a new Justice League is created in a lab.

REBIRTH

FINISH

The Crime Syndicate attacks Earth.

Darkseid dies during a battle with the Anti-Monitor. Jessica Cruz becomes a Green Lantern.

Wally West returns from the Speed Force. Heroes begin to remember previous realities.

The Justice League encounters the Kindred.

The spirit of the dead Superman and his replacement merge into one being.

Blue Beetle and Booster Gold awaken from a thousand-year stasis.

THE PANTHEON

Since the dawn of storytelling, epic tales of mythological beings have been told: divine entities, agents of good and evil, and forces of nature that assume human form. Like a latter-day pantheon of demigods, whose powers echo that of their mythic forebears, the Justice League faces incalculable odds and accomplishes impossible feats. While their nobility inspires and their unity transforms them into an invincible team, it is their humanity that makes these heroes truly powerful.

AQUAMAN

A man of land and sea, within Aquaman resides a primal power, a formidable force of nature. The oceans answer to his call, as do legions of undersea creatures. Aquaman is a king, yet often a reluctant hero, frequently torn between his loyalties to two worlds.

THE FLASH

The Flash's life is propelled by a silent need to push himself harder; to run further and faster than ever before. Swift enough to bend light, travel across time, and move through solid objects, he is also the League's beating heart; a messenger of hope even in the team's darkest hours.

WONDER WOMAN

Divine love and compassion given shape, Wonder Woman is the goddess of war and wisdom. Able to compel the truth from others and sway even her enemies' hardened hearts, she chooses violence only as a last resort, but is always prepared to lay down her life for her allies.

SUPERMAN

Strength incarnate, Superman is an unstoppable force who can soar beyond the heavens, melt steel, and move mountains. Energized by the sun and pure of heart, he has the power to shatter armies and conquer countries, yet elects to hide his identity and protect the undefended everywhere.

CYBORG

After his body was shattered in a terrible accident, pain and suffering defined this teenaged hero's life. Rebuilt with miraculous technology and wired to the world, Cyborg forges new tools and weaponry to handle any situation he encounters. Part-man, part-machine, he deploys the enhanced new capabilities he never wanted to help others.

GREEN LANTERN

Fuelled by an indomitable will, for Green Lantern weakness is never an option. Bestowed with a ring that enables him to control and solidify light, he can create anything he imagines. Yet his real power comes from his unflinching self-belief and faith in his own abilities.

BATMAN

Driven by righteous rage and an unquenchable thirst for justice, Batman needs no superpowers to achieve the impossible. Honing his body and mind to perfection, this stalker of the underworld forever risks his life to prevent others from experiencing the darkness that created him.

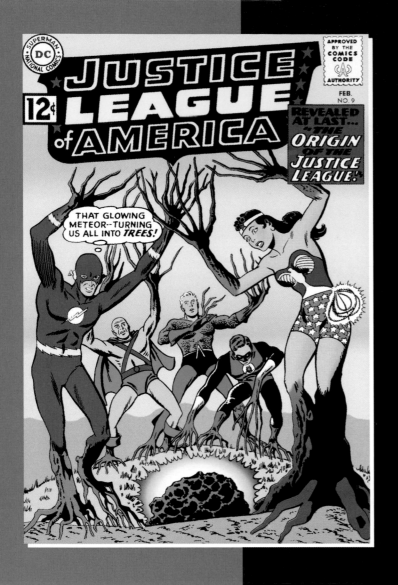

FEBRUARY 1962

MAIN CHARACTERS
Wonder Woman • Aquaman •
The Flash • Green Lantern •
Martian Manhunter • Batman •
Superman

SUPPORTING CHARACTERS
Green Arrow • Snapper Carr

MAIN LOCATIONS
Happy Harbor

JUSTICE LEAGUE OF AMERICA (VOL. 1) #9

THE HEROES OF EARTH COME TOGETHER AS A TEAM FOR THE FIRST TIME.

When a shape-shifting alien race decides to use the Earth as its battleground, the greatest heroes in the galaxy must join together to defend humanity. But can these heroes defeat a menace that can transform not only themselves but others as well?

1 Desperate to decide upon a new ruler and end their internal conflicts, the wisest of the alien race known as the Appellaxians settles on a course of action. Earth will serve as a suitable battleground for the seven beings that lay claim to the kingdom of Appellax.

2 Transformed into meteors and sent to Earth, each Appellaxian warlord awakes and begins mutating the population. They alter human bodies and assume control of their minds, with the intent of conquering the world.

"My hands and legs are turning to—solid diamond!"

BATMAN

3 One by one, the heroes of Earth face these elemental invaders, defeating their foes through incredible feats of power. Then tragedy strikes, as each hero in turn is ambushed by a wooden Appellaxian. They are transformed into trees and become unable to move of their own will.

4 The wooden Appellaxian believes it has vanquished Earth's defenders, unaware that he faces a combined power far beyond his own. Using their natural abilities, the heroes coordinate a maneuver that allows Wonder Woman to gain partial freedom. Taking advantage of the moment, the Amazon is able to easily destroy her attacker.

5 Seeking the final meteor, Wonder Woman, Aquaman, Green Lantern, The Flash, and the Martian Manhunter find Batman and Superman battling a diamond Appellaxian. Using his strength and speed, Superman changes the diamond body of the invader to coal, ending the threat of these evil alien warlords.

6 Deciding that they are stronger together than as individuals, the seven heroes declare themselves a team. They vow to use their great abilities to defend Earth, uphold the law, and vanquish evil: a united league dedicated to the cause of justice—the Justice League!

KEY CHARACTER

DATA FILE

REAL NAME: Kal-El/Clark Kent

FIRST APPEARANCE: *Action Comics* (Vol. 1) #1 (June 1938)

OCCUPATION: Reporter

AFFILIATIONS: Justice League, Legion of Super-Heroes

POWERS/ABILITIES: Flight, super-strength, super-speed, invulnerability, heat vision, X-ray vision, freeze breath, enhanced senses

SUNNY DISPOSITION

An eternal optimist, Clark Kent was raised by his adoptive parents to instinctively see the best in everyone, even his enemies. Thanks to this upbringing, as a hero, Superman makes it his mission to use his powers to serve all people, regardless of who or what they might be.

PIECES OF HOME

Soon after launching his career as the Man of Steel, Superman discovered that a mineral created from the destruction of his native world emitted toxic levels of radiation that mainly affected Kryptonians. This mineral became known as Kryptonite. It affects Superman in a variety of ways, depending on the color the alien crystal emits.

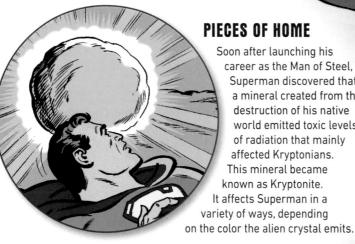

SYMBOL OF HOPE

Over the years that Superman has been active as a hero, his bright and colorful uniform, and his distinctive S-shield have become shining symbols that are highly regarded all across the galaxy. His name brings fear to warlords and hope to the downtrodden. This image of inspiration—a vision of peace, freedom, and justice for all—is a responsibility that the Man of Steel takes very seriously.

The S-shield on Superman's costume is the Kryptonian symbol for hope.

Superman's first uniform was made from the cloth in which the baby Kal-El came swaddled.

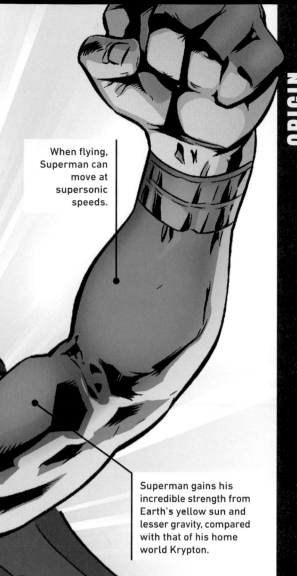

When flying, Superman can move at supersonic speeds.

Superman gains his incredible strength from Earth's yellow sun and lesser gravity, compared with that of his home world Krypton.

ORIGIN

Rocketed to Earth from the dying world of Krypton as an infant, Kal-El was discovered by a kindly couple named Jonathan and Martha Kent. Taking the baby as their own, they named him Clark Kent. He was raised unaware of his origins, slowly discovering that he was endowed with great powers far beyond those of any other mortal. Eventually, Clark's adoptive parents told their son the truth, revealing the rocket in which he was found. Choosing to use his amazing abilities for good, he became the hero known across the world as Superman.

"I'd rather good people trust me than bad people fear me."

SUPERMAN

MILD MANNERED

For many years, Superman lived his daily life under his adoptive name, Clark Kent. He chose to keep his identity a secret so that he could better serve the world and protect those near and dear to him. It has proven to be the right choice time and time again, as Clark's enemies have tried repeatedly to track down anyone close to Superman and use them against the Man of Steel.

SUPERMAN

Superman spent his early years as a solo hero, worried about the safety of anyone fighting alongside him and his ability to defeat his enemies while protecting allies. After witnessing the combined might of the Justice League during their first adventure, the Man of Steel realized he need not be concerned. He could fight side-by-side with formidable heroes who stood with one another as equals.

Designed to resemble a bat's wings, Batman's cape is made from memory cloth. An electrical signal activated from his right glove transforms the cape into gliding wings.

ORIGIN

As a young boy, Bruce Wayne witnessed the brutal murder of his parents at the hands of a petty thief called Joe Chill. From that moment on, Bruce vowed to spend his life and his fortune fighting injustice and waging ceaseless war on the criminal underworld.

In pursuit of his goals, Bruce traveled the globe, training in martial arts, science, and criminology to help him become a finely honed weapon of justice. However, he knew that this was not enough to strike fear into the hearts of the city's hardened and deadly criminals. Inspired by the bats that lived below Wayne Manor, he adopted the guise of this creature of the night and became Batman.

ASYLUM OF EVIL

Gotham City is home to the most evil and criminal minds imaginable. From the raw, brilliant madness of The Joker or the schizophrenic Two-Face, to the absurd obsessions of Mister Camera or the Dinosaur Gang, the Dark Knight continually faces both the worst and strangest foes around. Thanks to Batman's vigilance and peerless fighting skills, most of these dangerous felons end up doing time in the city's infamous institution for the criminally insane—the forbidding Arkham Asylum.

> "Criminals are a superstitious, cowardly lot..."
> — BATMAN

BATMAN

For years, the legendary Dark Knight operated in the shadows, cleaning Gotham City's streets of crime and corruption. But as the threats to the world grew, Batman stepped into the spotlight with the world's greatest heroes, ready to use his superb detective and combat skills to defend humanity from every conceivable crisis.

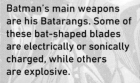

Batman's main weapons are his Batarangs. Some of these bat-shaped blades are electrically or sonically charged, while others are explosive.

Batman's cowl hides his identity and strikes terror into his enemies. A comms link in one of the ears helps him stay in touch with his allies and the G.C.P.D..

DATA FILE

REAL NAME: Bruce Wayne

FIRST APPEARANCE: *Detective Comics* (Vol. 1) #27 (May 1939)

OCCUPATION: Billionaire philanthropist

AFFILIATIONS: Justice League, Outsiders

POWWRS/ABILITIES: Unique deductive skills and fighting techniques; arsenal of non-lethal, hi-tech weaponry

Batman's Batsuit is made of bulletproof, fire-resistant synthetic fiber. The bat-symbol on his chest is designed to draw gunfire to the most heavily armored part of the suit.

LEGACY OF THE BAT

Although he prefers to work solo, the Dark Knight has assembled a team of allies—the "Batman Family"—to help combat crime. While Bruce Wayne's loyal butler Alfred Pennyworth works behind the scenes, Kate Kane, alias Batwoman, trains Red Robin, Spoiler, Orphan, and former villain Clayface to deal with any threat facing Gotham City. Batman can also call upon Robin (Damian Wayne), Red Hood, Nightwing, Batgirl, Duke Thomas and Batwing when needed.

READY FOR ANYTHING

Batman has no superpowers. He relies on his mind, body, and weapons to battle villains powerful enough to level a mountain. To that end, Bruce Wayne has spent a fortune devising tools that can be used to combat any foe, such as Batarangs, stun gauntlets, smoke grenades, knockout gas, and more. Above all, his grim determination helps him defeat overwhelming odds.

MASTER DETECTIVE

Batman is regarded as the World's Greatest Detective. His brilliant deductive mind is aided by an array of advanced technology he has at his fingertips. The highly sophisticated Batcomputer, based in the Batcave, has satellite links to monitor crisis points around the world. The Dark Knight also keeps a crime lab in his subterranean lair to help his investigations.

ORIGIN

Sculpted from clay and given life by the Gods, Princess Diana was raised as the only child of the Amazons, learning the arts of both healing and war. When a lone male pilot crashed on the shores of the island the Amazons call home, the Gods spoke to Diana's mother, Queen Hippolyta. The deities commanded the Amazon warriors to send an emissary to the outside world to help teach humanity the values of life and liberty that they were in danger of losing. A competition was held, at the end of which one contender stood triumphant—Princess Diana. She forsook her immortality and became the hero Wonder Woman.

TRIBAL RIVAL

When Hippolyta called for a new competition, Diana was forced to fight once more for the right to be Wonder Woman. This time, sabotaged by her mother, who sought to protect her daughter from danger, Diana lost. A new Wonder Woman was briefly named—Artemis of the lost tribe of Bana-Mighdall.

> *"Warriors, I ask you to join me in a fight to reclaim Heaven. Follow me... not as your princess... but as the God of War!"*
>
> WONDER WOMAN

CONFLICTING MEMORIES

There are many questions surrounding Wonder Woman's origins. While the Amazon remembers her history one way, there is evidence that another version of her own timeline once existed. In that timeline, she was the daughter of Zeus and ascended to the role of Goddess of War within the pantheon of deities that was her family.

DIPLOMATIC DUTIES

Unlike most of her allies, Wonder Woman has no secret identity, choosing to face all threats to the world in her role as Wonder Woman. However, not all of this time is spent battling evil as a Super Hero. The Amazon Princess is also a skilled diplomat, using her rank and royal station to negotiate treaties and spearhead humanitarian efforts around the globe.

WONDER WOMAN

Sent from the island paradise called Themyscira by the Greek Gods to spread a message of peace and freedom, Princess Diana was given the name Wonder Woman by the people of the world. Believing she could do more for humanity by allying herself with similarly powerful superhumans, the amazing Amazon became a founding member of the Justice League.

The indestructible silver gauntlets can deflect bullets and energy blasts.

DATA FILE

REAL NAME: Diana

FIRST APPEARANCE: *All Star Comics* (Vol. 1) #8 (Dec. 1941/Jan. 1942)

OCCUPATION: Princess, Ambassador

AFFILIATIONS: Justice League, Amazons of Themyscira

POWERS/ABILITIES: Flight, super-strength, limited invulnerability, enhanced speed, limited telepathy, enhanced reflexes

WARRIOR WOMAN

Though her mission is one of peace, Wonder Woman is well versed in the art of war. She does not hesitate to act against her enemies when the alternate option is the loss of innocent life. In this way, she often stands in conflict with some of her Justice League teammates, who tend to view the Amazon's warrior instincts with some discomfort.

Wonder Woman's shield is just one of the defensive and offensive Amazonian weapons in her armory.

The unbreakable Lasso of Truth compels anyone wrapped in its coils to tell the truth or obey the user's commands.

ORIGIN

The half-human, half-Atlantean son of a lighthouse keeper and a former queen of Atlantis, Arthur Curry was raised as a human by his father after his mother was forced to return to her undersea kingdom and wed another. Over the years, Arthur's Atlantean heritage asserted itself, allowing the young boy to breathe underwater and granting him phenomenal strength. Eventually embracing his true nature, Arthur journeyed to Atlantis and assumed his rightful place as heir and king, in the process usurping his younger half-brother, Orm (alias Ocean Master). In time, Arthur decided to abdicate his throne, choosing instead to dedicate himself full time to the role of a Super Hero.

"I couldn't turn my back on the world—I was a Super Hero long before I was a king."

Aquaman

ANCIENT MAGIKS

Over 145,000 years ago, Atlantean society was the pinnacle of civilization—a civilization that ultimately fell due to the influences of warring sorcerers. Though modern Atlantis is a culture that embraces science above sorcery, a brutal war between Aquaman and his half-brother, Orm, came dangerously close to reawakening the catastrophic magical powers once more.

POWER OF THE SEA

As many of Aquaman's adventures have taken place in the lost city of Atlantis, deep beneath the surface of the sea, much of humanity has come to vastly underestimate the raw strength of the sea king. In truth, while on land, Aquaman's strength, speed, and invulnerability rival those of his teammate Wonder Woman's, but underwater, none are truly his equal.

As well as being a weapon, the Trident of Neptune is a symbol of Atlantean royalty.

AQUAMAN

King of Atlantis and superhuman champion of Earth, Aquaman has had more difficulty than most dividing his time between his two demanding roles. Often the needs of Atlantis and the desires of the surface world have stood at odds, and it is only through his resolute will that the aquatic hero has struck a balance between these two disparate worlds.

Aquaman's great strength helps him to withstand the extreme pressures of the deep ocean.

Aquaman's unique telepathy allows him to command and communicate with sealife.

DATA FILE

REAL NAME: Arthur Curry

FIRST APPEARANCE: *More Fun Comics* (Vol. 1) #73 (Nov. 1941)

OCCUPATION: Monarch

AFFILIATIONS: Justice League, Kingdom of Atlantis, the Others

POWERS/ABILITIES: Capable of breathing underwater, super-strength, limited invulnerability, enhanced speed, limited telepathy

HOOKED

Prior to the universe-shaking events of Flashpoint, Aquaman temporarily lost his power to telepathically command marine life. Seizing his opportunity during a fierce fight, the amphibious villain Charybdis forced the Atlantean's arm into a river filled with piranha. Aquaman's hand was destroyed by the voracious fish, and for some time after the King of Atlantis used a high-tech harpoon in place of a hand.

FALLEN PRINCE

Pre-Flashpoint, Aquaman and his wife Mera had a son. Tragically, the child was kidnapped by Aquaman's nemesis, Black Manta, who used the toddler as a pawn in his war against Atlantis. In the process, the child was trapped inside a death machine and Aquaman was unable to save him.

Dorsal fins on Aquaman's costume assist his already unrivaled swimming abilities.

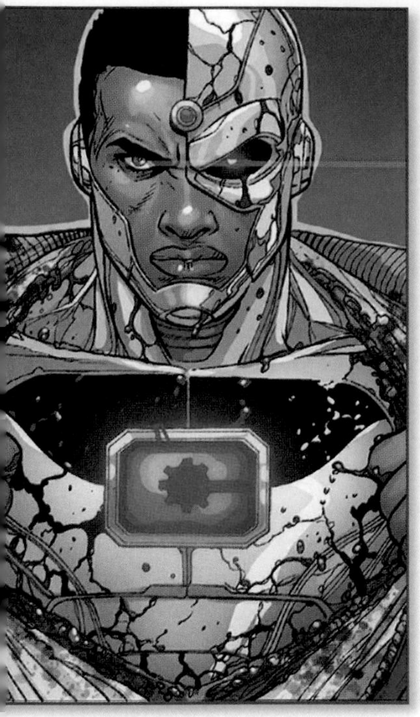

SACRIFICE

When his teammates were endangered by an Atlantean attack, Cyborg willingly sacrificed a remaining shred of his humanity—his lungs—so that he could be outfitted with an upgrade that would enable him to successfully survive underwater. It was a difficult decision for Victor, who felt that his connection with his human half was constantly slipping away.

ORIGIN

A star athlete at his high school, Victor Stone's body was almost completely destroyed when his scientist father tried experimenting with mysterious sentient computers from Apokolips. Furious at himself for the fate that had befallen his son, Victor's father dedicated all his scientific knowledge toward building a cybernetic body that could be used to give Victor life and purpose again. As a result, Dr. Stone succeeded in creating the most powerful cybernetic exoskeleton/life-support suit ever known. Although Victor originally had no interest in becoming a hero, it soon became impossible for him not to use his technologically-enhanced powers to save lives.

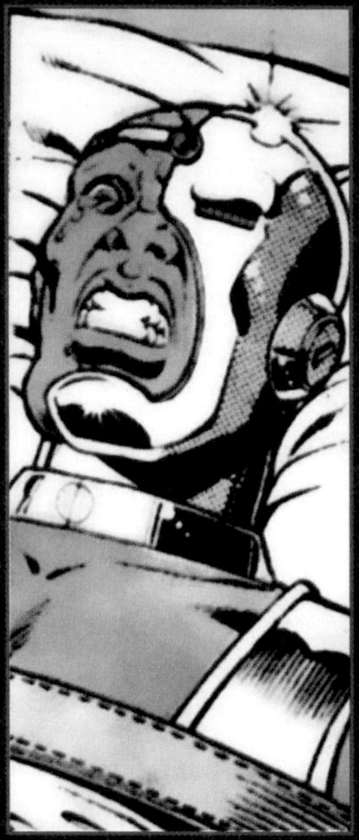

"Why couldn't you let me die?!"

CYBORG

EASY UPGRADE

Cyborg's technology is highly adaptive—meaning that it can easily absorb and learn from any other technologies that he encounters, upgrading itself as needed via an automatic process. This has come in handy on a great many occasions. It allows Victor Stone to physically alter the specifications of his mechanical anatomy to counter any new and unusual threats that he might come across in his battles against the forces of evil.

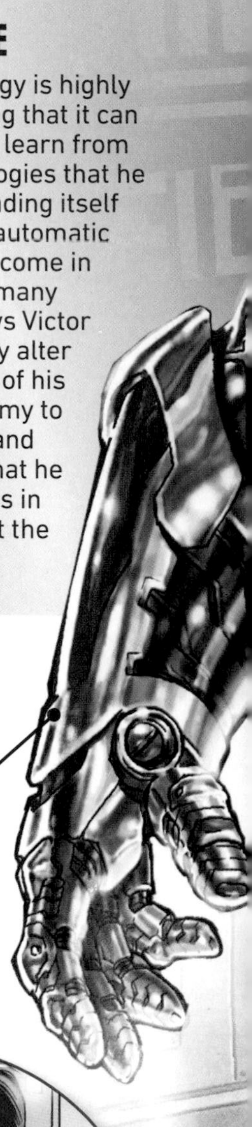

Cyborg's cybernetic enhancements also act as armor against energy blasts.

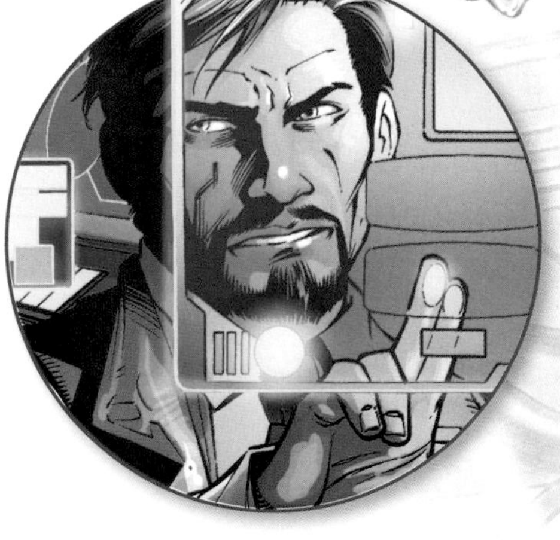

CYBORG

Victor Stone never wanted to be a Super Hero. Given the despair and rage he felt after his transformation, it would have been very easy for the young man to have followed a different, destructive path. Instead, he looked at the world and saw the potential good he could do as a hero.

TEAM EFFORT

Cyborg's father did not save Victor's life alone. He worked tirelessly with both S.T. A.R. Labs and several of the world's most brilliant robotic and cybernetic experts to create innovative technology that would allow his son to live and thrive. These experts included the renowned roboticist Dr. T.O. Morrow.

As well as enhanced eyesight, Cyborg's cybernetic left eye grants him infrared vision.

DATA FILE

REAL NAME: Victor Stone

FIRST APPEARANCE: *DC Comics Presents* (Vol. 1) #26 (Oct. 1980)

AFFILIATIONS: Teen Titans, Justice League, S.T.A.R. Labs

POWERS/ABILITIES: Super-strength, adaptive technology, technopathy, cybernetic senses, energy blasts, technomorphic healing factor, enhanced speed and agility, rocket-powered flight, electro-magnetic pulse and Boom Tube generation

ALTERED REALITY

Before the Flashpoint event—a reality-altering incident caused by The Flash attempting to change the past—Cyborg was not a member of the Justice League, but instead worked primarily with the Teen Titans. It was only after history was changed that Victor Stone became a founding member of the Justice League.

When Cyborg's defensive systems detect danger, his arm transforms into a white noise cannon.

DATA FILE

REAL NAME: Hal Jordan

FIRST APPEARANCE: *Showcase* (Vol. 1) #22 (Sep./Oct. 1959)

OCCUPATION: Test pilot

AFFILIATIONS: Justice League, Green Lantern Corps, Guardians of OA

POWERS/ABILITIES: Possesses an energy ring capable of creating hard light constructs based on thought and fueled by willpower

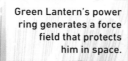

Green Lantern's power ring generates a force field that protects him in space.

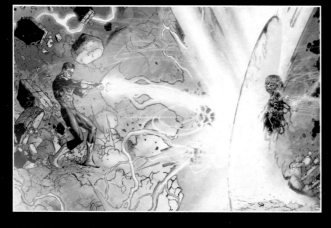

STRONG WILLED

The Green Lantern ring runs on pure willpower and, as such, Hal Jordan is a prime candidate for a power ring. He is confident to a fault, brash in his decision making, and has proven himself time and again to be heroic—to the point of being reckless with his own safety.

NATURAL LEADER

Having spent years learning to use his power ring, Hal Jordan is considered one of the most adept and powerful of all the Green Lanterns. As a result, he often finds himself in a leadership role during Corps missions. This is not so surprising, as it is rumored that even the renowned Guardians themselves have expressed a begrudging respect for Jordan's formidable abilities.

A Green Lantern's ring is considered among the most powerful weapons in the galaxy.

THE OATH

When the Green Lanterns recharge their ring, they traditionally recite an oath, one that pledges their allegiance to the Green Lantern Corps and the principals of the Guardians of OA.

"In brightest day, in blackest night, no evil shall escape my sight. Let those who worship evil's might, beware my power—Green Lantern's light!"

The Green Lantern Corps logo is an ancient symbol that stands for law and justice.

Even the uniform worn by Green Lantern is generated by his power ring.

When Abin Sur, the Green Lantern of Sector 2814, was struck down and mortally wounded, he sent his power ring—the weapon of the Green Lantern Corps—to find an individual who could overcome fear. Moments later, after scanning planet Earth, the ring determined that test pilot Hal Jordan was the nearest human worthy of the power and responsibility of a Green Lantern. Jordan was quickly transported by the remarkable ring to the side of Abin Sur. The dying alien tasked Jordan with carrying on his role as protector of Earth and all of Space Sector 2814.

"I hope to make Green Lantern a name to be feared by evildoers everywhere!"

GREEN LANTERN

SPECTRUM OF POWER

The energy of the Green Lanterns is but one aspect of the powerful spectrum of energy that can be drawn upon to sustain or destroy life. Red, yellow, blue, orange, violet, indigo, and black and white energies all sit on one side or the other of the spectrum, with green, the most balanced of these primordial energies, located at the center.

GREEN LANTERN

Hal Jordan is the protector of Space Sector 2814, which, due to the unique nature of life on Earth, has been the target of more alien invasions and cosmic crises than any other world. So much so that even a Green Lantern can use help protecting the populace, a role the Justice League is happy to fill.

DATA FILE

REAL NAME: Barry Allen

FIRST APPEARANCE: *Showcase* (Vol. 1) #4 (Sep./Oct. 1956)

OCCUPATION: Forensic scientist

AFFILIATIONS: Justice League

POWERS/ABILITIES: The ability to move at near light speed and phase through solid objects

When The Flash runs at super-speed, he can only be perceived as a scarlet blur.

MYSTERY MAN

Most people will never actually see what The Flash looks like, even when he's saving their lives. The Scarlet Speedster simply moves too fast for the human eye to follow. Even as he stands still, The Flash often vibrates at a high enough frequency that film does not capture his image. That blink-and-you'll-miss-it ability has made The Flash a mysterious hero who's always ready to save the day.

LEGACY OF SPEED

Due to the nature of his powers, The Flash has found himself at the center of more than one interdimensional crisis. On one occasion, after inadvertently losing himself in the extradimensional realm of the Speed Force, he was believed dead. In his absence, his sidekick Wally West discarded the identity of Kid Flash to become the new Flash.

On foot, The Flash can run at close to the speed of light—faster even than Superman.

While not superhumanly strong, The Flash can use his speed to boost his natural strength.

The Flash's whole costume compresses down into a ring on his finger.

ORIGIN

Barry Allen was struck by lightning while working in his laboratory late one stormy night, and was doused by a random mix of electrified chemicals. Miraculously unharmed, the young forensic scientist soon discovered that his cellular structure had somehow been changed. Always known to be perpetually slow and late, Barry Allen could now move so fast it was as if time around him was standing virtually still. After realizing he could use his amazing new powers to save lives, Barry fashioned a colourful costume for himself and became the heroic speedster known to the world as The Flash.

"A league against evil! Our purpose will be to uphold Justice!"

THE FLASH

QUICK THINKING

Barry Allen is so much more than just a speedster in a red suit. He is first and foremost a scientist. It is not uncommon for The Flash—who often faces villains who deploy scientific weapons and powers—to out-think his enemies using his scientific know-how rather than simply outrun them.

ALTERNATE DIMENSIONS

Early in his career, The Flash discovered that he could adjust the vibrations of his molecules. By doing this, he would alter the "frequency" of his existence, and shift from one version of reality to another. This allowed The Flash to explore parallel realities, and quickly brought him into contact with The Flash of another Earth— Jay Garrick. The two have teamed up on more than one occasion to combat multidimensional evil, before eventually inhabiting the same world.

THE FLASH

Though he calls Central City his home, The Flash's phenomenal speed allows him to divide his crime-fighting time across the entire world. Combining those abilities with his alter ego Barry Allen's easygoing collaborative nature, it's no surprise that the Fastest Man Alive is a team player. The Flash wasn't merely a founder of the original Justice League; he was also one of the first members to suggest the team name.

CHANGING NATURES

The Martian Manhunter's mood has been known to be as mercurial as his form. Though he is seen by most as a stern and unforgiving figure, to some he is perceived as compassionate and warm, sometimes even jovial.

The Manhunter is a complex individual, and no one, not even his teammates, truly knows every aspect of his nature.

ORIGIN

When the feared, warmongering White Martians conquered the civilization of the peaceful Green Martians, J'onn witnessed the death of his wife and child in a raging inferno. Shortly after, he was inadvertently transported across time and space to Earth. His home world of Mars was decimated, his people subjugated and eventually exterminated. With little choice in the matter, J'onn quietly accepted his fate and made a new life for himself, using his shape-shifting and mind-reading powers to create multiple secret identities that he could live under without detection.

ONCE BURNT

Martians have been known to be vulnerable to fire. Some have suggested that this weakness is a psychological limitation exclusive to the Martian Manhunter, due to the traumatic manner by which his family perished. However, it has been shown repeatedly that the related species known as the White Martians suffer from this weakness as well.

The Martian Manhunter's strength is comparable to that of Superman.

> *"There are 37 words for justice on Mars. There is no word for mercy."*
>
> **Martian Manhunter**

MARTIAN MANHUNTER

After spending decades alone on Earth, J'onn J'onnz had become distrustful of humanity, convinced that his true self would never be fully accepted. Though he spent his time in the shadows helping those in need, it wasn't until the Martian Manhunter began his association with the Justice League as a founding member that he finally found on Earth what he had long ago lost on Mars—a family.

A shape-shifter like all his kind, J'onn J'onzz seldom reverts to his true Martian form.

J'onn's Martian vision lets him project force beams and see many spectrums of light.

DATA FILE

REAL NAME: J'onn J'onzz

FIRST APPEARANCE: *Detective Comics* (Vol. 1) #225 (Nov. 1955)

OCCUPATION: Private investigator

AFFILIATIONS: Justice League, Stormwatch

POWERS/ABILITIES: Flight, super-strength, invulnerability, super-speed, optic force beams, enhanced senses, regenerative healing, telekinesis, telepathy, mind control, phasing, shape-shifting

KEEPING UP APPEARANCES

Martian physiology is less comparable to that of humans than J'onn's outward appearance might suggest. In truth, what most people see when they look at J'onn is no more his true form than any of his human disguises. The real Martian form is considerably more alien, and is something that J'onn understandably rarely chooses to share, even with his closest teammates.

COOKIE ADDICT

Due to a unique twist of Martian biology, J'onn finds certain types of foods mildly addictive—including crème-filled sandwich cookies. Despite his best efforts, the Martian Manhunter developed a fairly heavy dependency on this substance while functioning in the high stress position as team leader of the international branch of the Justice League.

THE MULTIVERSE

Countless millennia ago, there was only one reality—a single, linear existence. Then, Krona, a renegade Maltusian scientist obsessed with discovering the true nature of reality, linked the end of the universe with its beginning, resulting in a destructive surge of antimatter energy. This fractured existence into a multitude of parallel universes, each with its own distorted version of Earth.

THE JUSTICE SOCIETY

HAWKMAN

Carter Hall, alias the Hawkman of Earth-2, was the reincarnation of the long-dead Egyptian Prince Khufu, who was betrayed and murdered by the priest Hath-Set. When Carter's memories started to return, he took the identity of Hawkman and became a flying Super Hero.

DOCTOR MID-NITE

Blind surgeon Charles McNider discovered that, while blind in the light, he could now see in absolute darkness. Creating special goggles that prevented any light from entering, McNider armed himself with blackout bombs, and a bright red and green costume to fight crime as Doctor Mid-Nite.

HOURMAN

Biochemist Rex Tyler invented a vitamin that could imbue the user with superpowers for an hour. He tested the drug on himself, becoming the super-strong costumed adventurer Hourman. He later refined the dangerous drug to make it safe and only work for him.

THE FLASH

A college student exposed to chemical vapors in a campus laboratory, Jay Garrick gained the ability to move at supersonic speeds. Using these powers to save his future wife, Garrick donned his father's old war helmet and threw together a quick costume, becoming The Flash.

The Justice League exists on Earth-1—though their reality is not the first. The name was given by that world's inhabitants as they charted their place within the ever-shifting sea of parallel universes. Earth-1's closest neighbor is called Earth-2, home of the Justice Society, a team of heroes assembled to battle for freedom and liberty.

The Justice Society and the Justice League shared many adventures, until the Crisis event occurred where all universes were merged into one. With their history rewritten, the heroes of the many Earths merged with their counterparts, and all beings now existed on one singular world.

Eventually, the multiverse would regrow, subtly different from before. Time and again, the never-ending cycle of death and rebirth occurs. Each time, the heroes of the multiverse find themselves reimagined, their very life forces manipulated by an impossibly powerful being who exists outside all boundaries.

SANDMAN

It was the recurring nightmares that drove Wesley Dodds, a millionaire playboy, to don a gas mask and hunt down criminals with his special sleeping gas gun. Unknown to the hero, his dreams were caused by the imprisonment of one of the Endless—the living manifestation of dreams.

THE ATOM

Al Pratt was a small man who, tired of being bullied, trained himself to become a formidable fighting force. His efforts were very successful, and the young college sophomore-turned-pint-sized powerhouse took the codename The Atom and soon became a member of the Justice Society.

STARMAN

Astronomer Ted Knight invented a special gravity rod that enabled him to fly and to weaponize starlight energy. Convinced by his cousin to become a Super Hero, the scientist warily began a new costumed career as Starman, fighting criminals alongside the Justice Society.

GREEN LANTERN

Discovering a magic green lamp carved from a fallen meteorite, Alan Scott, a young engineer, managed to harness the power of the mystical artifact to save a train from derailing. Carving a matching ring from the curious metal, he became Green Lantern, protector of Gotham City.

CRIME SYNDICATE

The Crime Syndicate hails from a parallel reality, Earth-3, where evil always wins. These twisted doppelgängers of the Justice League long ago conquered their own world, and now seek to expand their criminal empire by invading other realities—a resolute mission that has been thwarted at every turn by the Justice League.

POWER RING

Chosen to wield the Ring of Volthoom because he was weak-willed and cowardly, Harold Jordan soon found his life ruled by another: the ring itself. Enslaved, Harold loses a little bit of his life force every time he uses the ring—and he has no choice but to use the ring. After his death, the power ring located Jessica Cruz as its new host. She eventually became a member of the Green Lantern Corps.

ULTRAMAN

Rocketed from Krypton so that he could conquer those that destroyed his homeworld, young Kal-Il was sent forth with the message to become the strongest there is— or be nothing at all. The inverse of Superman, Ultraman gains power through exposure to Kryptonite.

OWLMAN

When his mother and younger brother Bruce were gunned down by a policeman, Thomas Wayne, Jr. blamed his father. Dedicating his life to avenging himself against the law and his father, Thomas became Owlman, the brilliant and morally bankrupt tactician of the Crime Syndicate.

SUPERWOMAN

This Amazon traveled to the world ruled by men to prove her superiority. Taking the alias of Lois Lane, Superwoman quickly took control of the *Daily Planet*, ruling the corporation as if it were her own private kingdom, all the while terrorizing the innocent as Superwoman.

GRID

Originally a passive subroutine that was a part of the hero Cyborg's unique programming, Grid's purpose was to monitor all super-powered beings on Earth. Upon becoming sentient, Grid craved and was given a body of its own—a reward promised to the malevolent artificial intelligence by the Crime Syndicate.

ATOMICA

While escaping from the police with her partner in crime, Jonathan Allen, Rhonda Pineda fell into the laboratory of Ray Palmer's size-manipulating Atomico project at S.T.A.R. Labs. As a result, she was inadvertently granted the power to shrink down to microscopic size.

DEATHSTORM

A scientist known for experimenting on humans, Martin Stein was captured by enemies of the Crime Syndicate. Using the lab he was imprisoned in to experiment on himself, he fused his body with a victim that he could control, and became Deathstorm.

JOHNNY QUICK

A professional criminal, Jonathan Allen was pinned down by the police on the roof of S.T.A.R. Labs with his partner Rhonda Pineda. Johnny was struck by lightning trying to escape, and was given the ability to move at near-light speed.

THE OUTSIDER

Alfred Pennyworth, a poverty-stricken genius who was given purpose by Owlman, has served his master with unswerving loyalty for many years. Even after being captured and poisoned by the Earth-3 version of the Joker, the Outsider always remains ready and able to do Owlman's bidding.

AMAZO

Considered one of the first true artificial beings, Amazo is constructed of synthetic organic tissue that mimics the composition of a human being down to the cellular level. With no real purpose beyond wreaking havoc upon the Justice League, the android has proven to be one of the most dangerous foes the heroes have ever faced.

ORIGIN

An artificial being able to duplicate the abilities of anyone it encounters, Amazo was created by Professor Ivo to overcome the Justice League so that Ivo could continue his quest for immortality without interference. Difficult to defeat due to its unique power and unpredictable nature, Amazo continually returns to threaten the world. It does so either in its original artificial body, or through new forms designed to host its sinister consciousness.

"You are easily outmatched. I will end this quickly."

AMAZO

KILLER VIRUS

Perhaps Amazo's deadliest attack came when its artificial DNA was uploaded into nanobots and transformed into a lethal, unstable virus. The virus infected thousands of victims, stripping superhumans of their powers, while turning humans into metahumans before violently killing them. Many members of the Justice League were affected—including Batman, who turned into a monstrous bat creature—before Lex Luthor found a cure in Superman's Kryptonian antibodies.

Amazo's adaptive body absorbs the powers of any being in his vicinity.

Once absorbed, Amazo can retain another being's power, be it Superman's strength or the Flash's speed.

DATA FILE

ALIASES: Timazo, Humazo, Hourmazo

FIRST APPEARANCE: *The Brave and the Bold* (Vol. 1) #30 (Jun./Jul. 1960)

AFFILIATIONS: Secret Society of Super-Villains, O Squad, Injustice League

POWERS/ABILITIES: Power mimicry

KANJAR RO

The Justice League first encountered the dictator known as Kanjar Ro when they were kidnapped and forced to participate in a planetary war on the world of Dhor. Kanjar Ro hoped to use the League as weapons against his rivals. Defeated and removed from power, the dictator has returned on many occasions, seeking either to regain his former authority and dominance, or wreak revenge on the League. Despite his malevolent ambitions, Kanjar Ro has been known to work with the heroes when confronting a common enemy.

STARRO

An alien life form bent on enslaving other races through its telepathic hive-mind, Starro spreads across the galaxy like a plague. The creature generates star-shaped spores that attach themselves to victims and subvert their will. Able to regrow its entire being from a single cell, Starro has proven to be a virtually indestructible threat to the Justice League. It has even managed to spread its consciousness across dimensions. The entity appears to exist in multiple forms at once, some of which can grow as large as a continent.

DESPERO

Despero was born a mutant on the world of Kalanor, where he used the psionic powers granted him by his third eye to enslave and rule his people. Brought to the remote planet by a group of desperate rebels, the Justice League helped overthrow the monstrous tyrant. Seeking revenge, Despero submitted his body to nuclear energy, which mutated him even further. Now more powerful and more savage, he seeks to cause pain and misery on any world upon which he sets foot—most of all Earth, home to the heroes who thwarted his ambitions.

ALIEN INVADERS

Despite Earth being under the protection of the galaxy's greatest heroes, would-be interstellar conquerors have made it clear that they view humanity as their personal playthings.

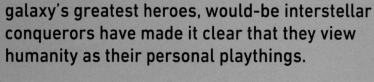

DIABOLICAL AND DEADLY

The threats the newly formed Justice League encountered were not limited to enemies attacking from alternate worlds or outer space. An increasing number of homegrown, volatile villains deployed technology and supernatural means to combat the League and run rampant across the globe.

> "Soon the Black Baptism will unleash the demonic hordes to feed upon the cattle of humanity."
>
> FELIX FAUST

DOCTOR DESTINY

John Dee was an inventor who fought Green Lantern with deadly antigravity devices and machines developed to weaken willpower. He truly became Doctor Destiny when he created the Materioptikon, an apparatus that allowed its user to manipulate the dreams of others. The device was powered by a stone that once belonged to the Sandman—the embodiment of dreams. However, prolonged use of the device drove Dee insane. In time, the Sandman reclaimed his stone, but despite this loss, Doctor Destiny found that years of exposure had imbued him with the powers he had once fabricated. He continued his criminal rampages.

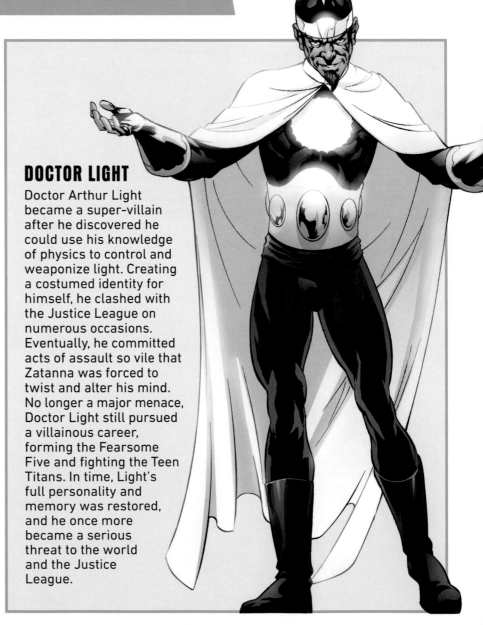

DOCTOR LIGHT

Doctor Arthur Light became a super-villain after he discovered he could use his knowledge of physics to control and weaponize light. Creating a costumed identity for himself, he clashed with the Justice League on numerous occasions. Eventually, he committed acts of assault so vile that Zatanna was forced to twist and alter his mind. No longer a major menace, Doctor Light still pursued a villainous career, forming the Fearsome Five and fighting the Teen Titans. In time, Light's full personality and memory was restored, and he once more became a serious threat to the world and the Justice League.

FELIX FAUST

Originally from around 5000 BC, the true name of this evil sorcerer is long since lost in the mists of time. Banished by a rival into an alternate dimension, this unnamed wizard languished in limbo until the early 20th century, when a magician, Dekan Drache, found a way to release the ancient being. Taking Drache's body as his own, the necromancer discovered his powers were greatly diminished. He thus began a quest to regain them by bargaining with devils. Adopting the name Felix Faust, the villain soon gained the attention of the Justice League, who have thwarted his pursuit for ultimate power on many occasions.

ROYAL FLUSH GANG

Originally formed by Amos Fortune from the remnants of his childhood band of friends, the Royal Flush Gang is a group of five criminals dressed as playing cards. They used Fortune's technology to commit crimes. At first led by the boastful Fortune himself in the guise of Ace, the team went through many changes, and all the original members were eventually replaced. For a brief time, the gang was associated with a villain they believed to be the Joker, who instead turned out to be an imposter by the name of the Gambler.

THE DEMONS THREE

Abnegazar, Rath, and Ghast are the known names of these three demonic entities, who claim to have once been galactic rulers. Time and again the three demons have attempted to manipulate mortals into freeing them from their banishment. To accomplish this, their essences have been tethered to three mystical artifacts: the Green Bell of Uthool, the Silver Wheel of Nyorlath, and the Red Jar of Calythos. The Demons Three first encountered the Justice League when Felix Faust attempted to use their demonic powers to regain his own lost sorcery.

Dedicated to fighting injustice and righting wrongs, the seven most powerful heroes of Earth made history when they unified under one banner. Resolved to serve all mankind, they became the legendary Justice League of America.

THE EARLY YEARS

JLA (Vol. 1) #7 (Oct./Nov. 1961)
The Justice League goes undercover at
a carnival to save the Earth.

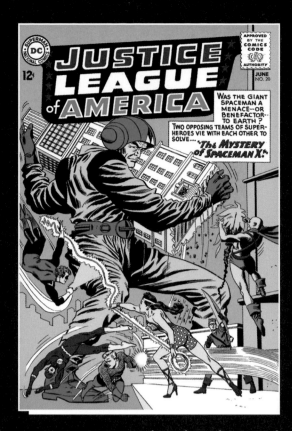

JLA (Vol. 1) #20 (Jun. 1963)
Unable to defeat a giant robot in battle, the
Justice League must find the source of its power.

JLA (Vol. 1) #21 (Aug. 1963)
Reaching across dimensions,
the Justice League meets the
Justice Society for the first time.

JLA (Vol. 1) #75 (Nov. 1969)
Having just joined the team,
Black Canary demonstrates her
devastating sonic scream powers.

SECRET SANCTUARY

After the formation of the Justice League, the super-team set about establishing a headquarters for themselves. Needing a location that was both private and easily accessible, the fledgling group decided to set up base in a previously undiscovered cave deep within a mountain in Happy Harbor, Rhode Island.

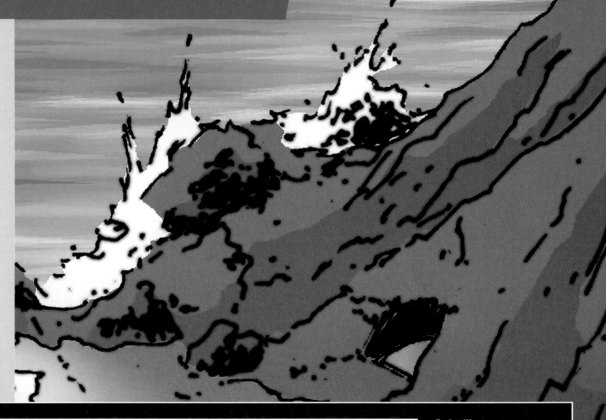

MEMBERS

Superman

Batman

Wonder Woman

The Flash

Green Lantern

Martian Manhunter

Aquaman

Green Arrow

The Atom

Hawkman

Black Canary

Early allies
Still in its infancy, the Justice League's roster changed very little during the team's time in the Secret Sanctuary. The original seven members were joined by new heroes, such as Green Arrow, The Atom, Hawkman, and Black Canary, and all remained fully committed to the cause and team.

COMFORTS OF HOME

With funds donated by billionaires Bruce Wayne (Batman) and Oliver Queen (Green Arrow), the Justice League of America was able to build a state-of-the-art headquarters. Equipped with high-tech crime labs, a gymnasium, a well-stocked library, and an aircraft hangar, the Secret Sanctuary was more than ready to meet any needs and adapt to any conceivable emergency.

LAST LAUGH

Eventually, Snapper Carr, the League's unofficial mascot, was manipulated into betraying the location of the Secret Sanctuary to the Joker. In response, the Justice League abandoned their headquarters. Over time, the mountain hideout became home to a variety of new tenants. Young Justice, the Doom Patrol, and later incarnations of the JLA all turned the League's former base into their own sanctuaries.

A MULTIVERSE IN CRISIS

Outside the boundaries of the universe exists the endless multiverse, which encompasses parallel realities, each mirroring the next in almost perfect detail. It is on these alternate Earths that the Justice League has had some of its most amazing adventures—and fought some of its deadliest foes.

Justice League of America (Vol. 1) #30 (Sep. 1964)
The Justice League battles its evil counterpart, the Crime Syndicate.

Justice League of America (Vol. 1) #21 (Aug. 1963)
Introductions are made and alliances forged, as the Justice League and the Justice Society meet for the first time.

CRISIS ON EARTH-3

Looking for a new challenge, the vicious and undefeated Crime Syndicate of America sets its sights on the universe of the Justice League. Concerned that they risk failure outside their own universe, the Syndicate summons the League to its own evil universe, entrapping the team. After the Syndicate similarly defeats the JSA, the JLA returns and imprisons the villainous doppelgängers in the vibrational space that exists between realities.

CRISIS ON EARTH-X

Transported to a world where Hitler and the Axis powers won WWII, the JLA and the JSA team up with Uncle Sam and his Freedom Fighters. During the mission, the heroes are turned against each other, each side desperate to win to save the world. The chaos only ends when Red Tornado discovers a Nazi mind-control station orbiting in space, which he must single-handedly destroy if Earth-X is ever to know peace.

CRISIS ON TWO EARTHS

When villains from the parallel Earth of the Justice Society team up with three of the Justice League of America's greatest foes, the JLA is rendered helpless. Down but not out, the League use the magic ball of Merlin to breach the dimensional barrier between worlds and unite with the JSA. It proves to be a sound strategy, as it soon becomes clear that the only way to win the day is for the multiverse's two greatest Super Hero teams to combine forces.

Justice League of America (Vol. 1) #107 (Sep./Oct. 1973)
Uncle Sam leads the Freedom Fighters—Doll Man, Phantom Lady, the Ray, Black Condor, and the Human Bomb—against Nazi troops in America.

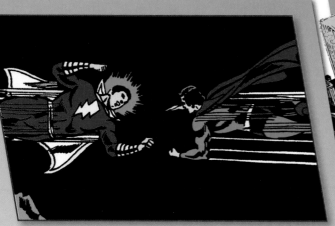

Justice League of America (Vol. 1) #137 (Dec. 1976)
Captain Marvel cries "Shazam!" as he rockets toward Superman, hoping his magic lightning will bring the Man of Steel to his senses.

CRISIS ON EARTH-S

When several villains from multiple realities unite to displace the Elders—gods who give the Shazam Family their magical powers—the JLA and the JSA team up with the Squadron of Justice from Earth-S. This planet has been trapped by a bizarre and unnatural eclipse, caught between perpetual night and endless day. After a furious battle, the villains are all defeated, but Captain Marvel has to use his magic lightning to stop a rampaging, mind-controlled Superman.

CRISIS ON INFINITE EARTHS

A cosmic threat beyond the scope of any ever encountered by the League rises from the depths of the Antimatter Universe: the Anti-Monitor, a being that consumes realities. Using his great power for destruction, the Anti-Monitor tears across existence. Only the combined heroic forces of every incarnation of Earth have a hope of stopping him. Ultimately, all realities and Earths are merged into one, and for a time, the multiverse becomes one single universe.

Crisis on Infinite Earths (Vol. 1) #12 (Mar. 1986)
The final conflict with the all-powerful Anti-Monitor involves heroes from across the multiverse.

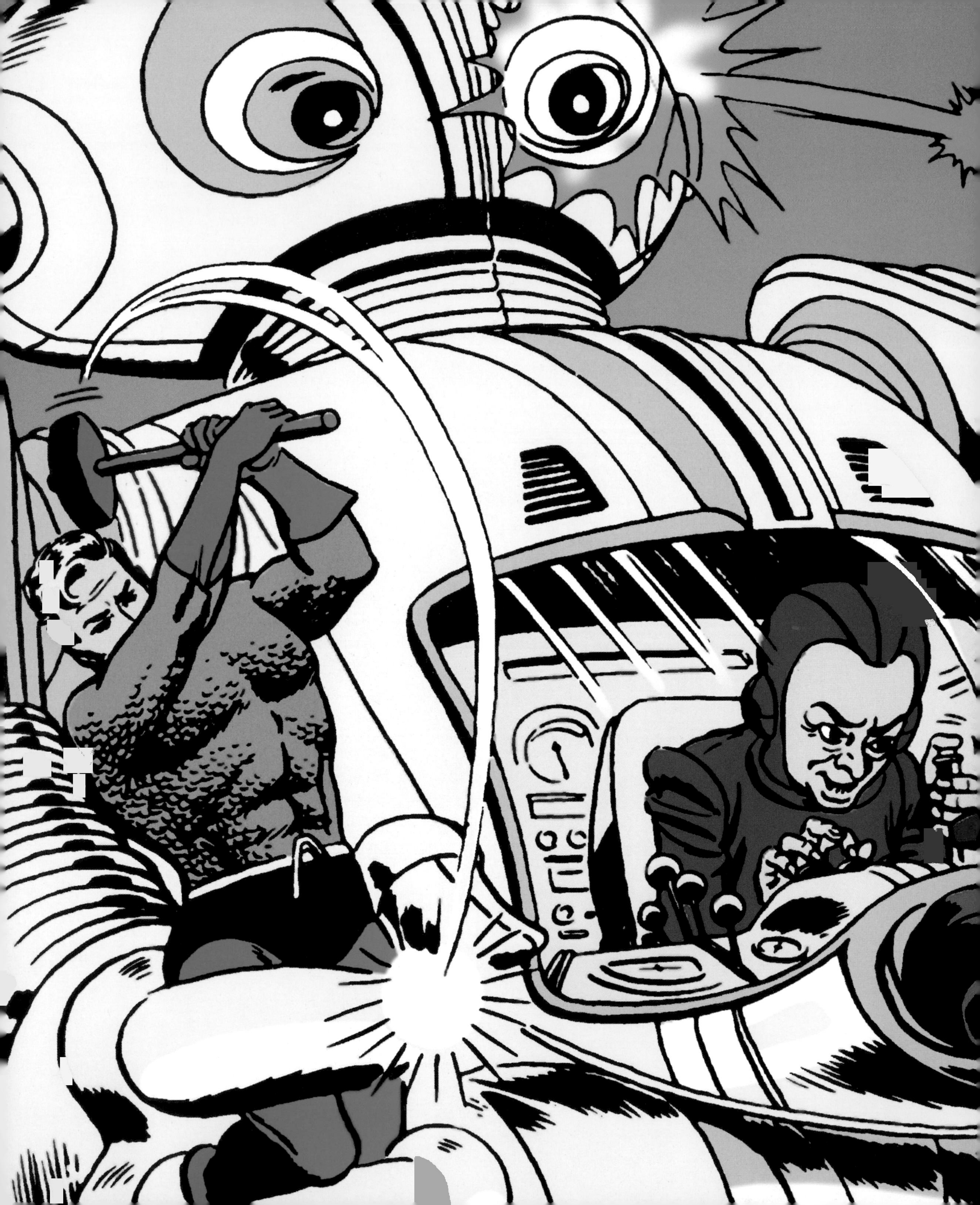

The Brave and the Bold (Vol. 1)
#29 (April/May 1960)
The Weapons Master journeys to the past to avoid capture by the Intersolar Police. His plan: to use his weapons to defeat the Justice League, thus learning which tools will be most effective when fighting the law in his own time.

BIGGER AND BOLDER

Shortly after the team's formation, it became clear that the Justice League could do more good by expanding its membership. Within months, several new members joined the ranks of the planet's mightiest, adding their substantial combined abilities to that of the World's Greatest Super Heroes.

> "Sure, it teaches you how to protect, but from the very start— the League teaches you how to fight."
>
> GREEN ARROW

GREEN ARROW

After being shipwrecked on a deserted island, Oliver Queen was forced to rely solely on his hunting skills to survive. Over the years that he was lost, he diligently trained himself to become an expert archer. By the time he was rescued from the island, the billionaire playboy had become the most adept bowman on the planet. Once he was home, the former castaway became determined to use his vast wealth and newfound skills in archery and hand-to-hand combat to fight crime and corruption.

THE ATOM

While studying technologies he hoped would help address food shortages, Ray Palmer used a rare white dwarf star alloy to invent a device that could shrink any object it was focused on. Unfortunately, it also caused anything it shrunk to explode after an hour. Though he had given up hope of making the device work, Palmer was forced to use it on himself to save his students after a cave collapsed. Inspired to become a hero, Palmer became the size-changing crime fighter known as The Atom, and joined the Justice League soon after his first adventure.

SNAPPER CARR

This honorary member of the Justice League was invariably close to the action whenever the Super Heroes raced into battle. Helping out however he could—often by contacting Leaguers when he spotted trouble—Snapper Carr quickly became a regular fixture on the team. Over time, his relationship with the League put a strain on Snapper, who felt that he was only defined by the heroes who surrounded him. He was tricked by The Joker into betraying the Justice League, and disappeared in disgrace. Some time later, he briefly became a hero himself after gaining the power to teleport at the snap of his fingers. Eventually, he wrote a memoir of his experiences, but he was never able to shake off the guilt that he felt over his betrayal of his friends and allies.

BLACK CANARY

The original Black Canary, Dinah Drake, was born on the parallel world known as Earth-2. After a tragic adventure in which her husband, Larry Lance, was killed, Dinah decided to make her home on Earth-1, switching from the Justice Society to the Justice League during a cosmic team-up between the two groups. Soon after, Black Canary developed a powerful sonic scream, one that made the already skilled vigilante an even more potent Super Hero. Eventually, Dinah Drake was revealed to have died with her husband in the accident. It was, in fact, her daughter, Dinah Laurel Lance, who had journeyed to Earth-1 in her mother's stead to become the new Black Canary.

HAWKMAN

Katar Hol (aka Hawkman) is an intergalactic policeman from the distant planet Thanagar, who uses a winged antigravity harness to fly. Though he originally traveled to Earth in pursuit of a shape-shifting super-villain named Byth, the winged hero soon decided it was his duty to remain on Earth to help humanity control its dangerous criminal element. Taking the name of Carter Hall and disguising himself as an archaeological linguist—one that specialized in ancient weapons and warfare—it wasn't long before Katar joined the growing ranks of the Justice League.

ZATANNA'S SEARCH

With the heroes of the Justice League operating publicly, it was inevitable that they would draw the attention of other, similarly powered beings. Enter Zatanna, a young woman of mysterious origin in desperate need. One by one, the Justice Leaguers will aid this magic-wielding wizardress on her quest to find one dear to her heart...

Hawkman (Vol. 1) #4 (Oct./Nov. 1964)
Hawkman's investigations take him to China, where he is alarmed to find a motionless girl seemingly speaking in tongues.

SEEING DOUBLE

While investigating the mysterious appearance of artifacts in the Midway City Museum, Hawkman encounters a weird immobile woman speaking in a strange language. Half a world away, his wife, Hawkgirl, comes across the same frozen figure. When the heroes unite, the two strange doppelgängers become one. The woman is revealed as the magician Zatanna, who is on a mission to find her long-missing father, the spell-casting crime-fighter Zatara.

The Atom (Vol. 1) #19 (Jun./Jul. 1965)
Zatanna and The Atom shrink ever-smaller, tumbling through the gaps between molecules on their quest to find Zatara.

DANGEROUS DRUID

Continuing her search, Zatanna encounters The Atom. The pair take a journey to a world that exists inside a subatomic particle. In this domain, they find a magical kingdom ruled by an evil druid who confesses that he used his powers to send Zatara to an unknown realm. Before they can learn more, the druid is rendered comatose by his own evil hand.

Detective Comics (Vol. 1) #355 (Sep. 1966)
Seeking the Golden Ting Tripod to help her locate Zatara, Zatanna has a run-in with a gangster.

"Who Arataz raeppa ot em!"

ZATANNA

WICKED WARLOCK

Undeterred, Zatanna tries to locate her lost father in the sub-dimensional land of Ys, a place on the other side of reality, formed from the excess energy of the original Big Bang. Ensnared by the Warlock of Ys, Zatanna is taken prisoner, along with Justice Leaguer Green Lantern. Teaming up to escape, the pair discover that the Warlock is seeking revenge on Zatara, who has stolen his crystal ball. The heroes flee, and Zatanna vows to continue her quest.

Green Lantern (Vol. 2) #42 (Jan. 1966)
Dispatched by the Warlock of Ys, weapon-wielding warriors and destructive demons attack Green Lantern and Zatanna.

MIGHT OVER MAGIC

Searching for a magical golden tripod to help find her father, Zatanna crosses paths with a gang of thieves who are being hunted by Elongated Man. In her encounter with the crooks, Zatanna's magic is neutralized by a mystical book of dark power. Luckily, her hand-to-hand fighting skills, along with assistance from Elongated Man, are more than enough to defeat the gangsters. Retrieving the tripod—as well as the arcane book—Zatanna plans to journey to a realm of darkness, where she believes she will find her father.

Justice League of America (Vol. 1) #51 (Feb.1967)
The League receives Zatanna's thanks—and her grateful hugs.

BROKEN SPELLS

Zatanna's search comes to an end when she reaches the enchanted land of Kharma, aided by a spirit named Allura. Empowered, Zatanna summons the heroes she met during her long quest, including Batman, who she had earlier secretly met. After helping her fight all manner of strange adversaries, the heroes deduce the truth—that Zatanna has actually been possessed by Allura, and that her evil spirit must be exorcized. In the process, a curse that had kept Zatara locked away is broken, and father and daughter are at last reunited—thanks to the Justice League.

EARLY ENCOUNTERS

The Justice League formed to oppose threats beyond the measure of any one hero. It is no surprise, then, that some of the most dangerous and vile criminals of the underworld would come out of the shadows so soon after the team formed.

APPELLAXIANS

The Appellaxians are a warlike race of aliens who once sought to transform the population of Earth into armies. They gave up their quest for war after their humiliating defeat at the hands of the newly formed Justice League.

WEAPONS MASTER

Xotar, the Weapons Master from the distant future, once obtained an ancient diary belonging to Snapper Carr. The diary revealed that the villain was destined to travel back in time and battle the Justice League on several occasions.

ECLIPSO

Also known as the God of Vengeance, the entity that is Eclipso is trapped inside a gem called the Heart of Darkness. Whenever someone comes into contact with this gem, the mind of Eclipso can influence them and even take complete control of their body. Through this physical form Eclipso is able to wield extraordinary supernatural powers.

T.O. MORROW

Thomas Oscar Morrow, aka Tomek Ovadya Morah, is a genius robotics expert obsessed with perfecting artificial life. As a scientist, he is less concerned with villainy and more interested in discovery, no matter what the cost. His greatest achievement is the creation of the self-aware artificial intelligence known as Red Tornado.

QUEEN BEE

Zazzala of the hive-world Korll is driven by one burning desire—the expansion of her empire. Using a variety of mind-controlling powers, Queen Bee has troubled the Justice League on several occasions, most typically using potent pheromones to enslave the male members of the team.

SHAGGY MAN

A synthetic being infused with the DNA of a salamander, the barely aware creature of rage that is Shaggy Man is strong enough to stand against Superman. He can also heal at a speed that is impossible to calculate.

LORD OF TIME

A feared warlord from the year 3786, Epoch is a powerful manipulator of the timestream, who uses a chrono-cube to explore the fourth dimension. Along the way, the self-proclaimed Lord of Time has often tried to raise armies and change history, and has proven to be a persistent thorn in the side of the Justice League. Born in the 38th century, Epoch chooses to base himself in the year 1,000,000,000.

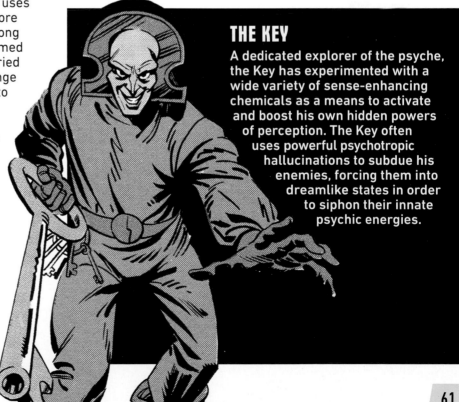

THE KEY

A dedicated explorer of the psyche, the Key has experimented with a wide variety of sense-enhancing chemicals as a means to activate and boost his own hidden powers of perception. The Key often uses powerful psychotropic hallucinations to subdue his enemies, forcing them into dreamlike states in order to siphon their innate psychic energies.

TEEN TITANS

Before Robin and the rest of the Teen Titans became a Super Hero team, they were a band of friends with one thing in common: they were all junior sidekicks of members of the Justice League. This group of kids became an official crime-fighting team when their mentors began exhibiting odd, criminal behavior. It was up to Robin, Kid Flash, Speedy, Aqualad, and Wonder Girl to set things right.

> *"What's this...?*
> *Calling the*
> *'Teen Titans'?"*
> BATMAN

JUNIOR JUSTICE

When the Justice League inexplicably turned to crime, their younger sidekicks banded together to stop them, each taking on another's mentor to maintain the element of surprise. Robin, Speedy, Wonder Girl, Kid Flash, and Aqualad eventually learned that the League members were being mind-controlled by an evil alien parasite. After defeating the League—and the parasite—the young heroes formed a league of their own—the Teen Titans.

AQUALAD

Born to a remote Atlantean tribe, Garth was cast out because his purple eye color was seen as a sign of dark magic. Surviving alone for years, he was discovered by Aquaman who, as King of Atlantis, took the boy under his wing as Aqualad. Like his mentor, Garth can breathe underwater and is far stronger than the average human. He also possesses magical abilities, though when he joined the original Teen Titans, he lacked the training to use them.

ROBIN

Circus acrobat Dick Grayson was orphaned after a crime boss sabotaged his parents' trapeze line. Adopted by billionaire Bruce Wayne, the young boy became Batman's protégé, battling the worst criminals in Gotham City as Robin. Grayson received peerless crime-fighting training, which he combined with his own exceptional acrobatic talents. This soon placed him in the ranks of the most skilled martial artists in the world, second only to his mentor.

SPEEDY

The orphaned son of a forest ranger, Roy Harper was raised by a Navajo chief, who trained him to be an expert archer. As a teenager, Roy was obsessed with the hero Green Arrow, and soon secured a role as the Emerald Archer's hot-headed sidekick. Roy joined the Teen Titans soon after their formation, but found it quite difficult to fully commit to the young team.

WONDER GIRL

When she was just a toddler, young Donna was rescued from a fire by Wonder Woman and given sanctuary on Paradise Island. Here she was endowed with powers similar to those of her adoptive Amazon sisters. As she grew into a teenager, the young woman adopted the identity of Wonder Girl in honor of her older sister, Diana. Moving back to the US, the younger heroine found a surrogate family with the Teen Titans and took the civilian name of Donna Troy.

KID FLASH

Teenager Wally West had long admired the Central City hero the Flash. When a lightning bolt struck Wally, replicating the accident that gave the Flash his amazing speed, Barry Allen revealed his identity as the Fastest Man Alive to his new super-speed protégé. The two swiftly became inseparable.

As humanity reached beyond the limitations of Earth and began to climb to the stars, the Justice League shifted its role to that of global protectors. The expanded team stood ready to defend the planet against any and all threats from the depths of space.

COSMIC DEFENDERS

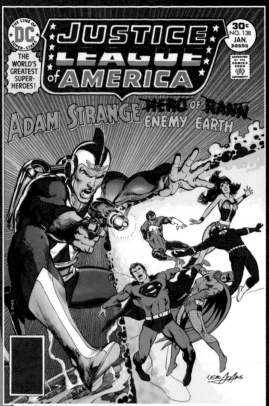

***JLA* (Vol. 1) #138 (Jan. 1977)**
The Justice League must save Adam Strange
from zeta-beam madness.

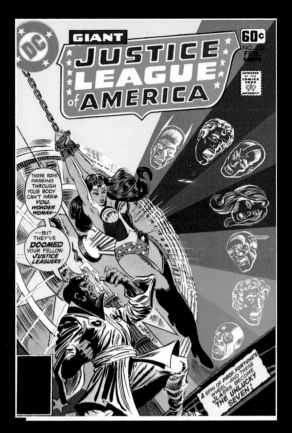

***JLA* (Vol. 1) #151 (Feb. 1978)**
Amos Fortune devises a plan to steal the
powers of the Justice League.

***JLA* (Vol. 1) #178 (May 1980)**
In an effort to save his people,
the Martian Manhunter is forced to
play a deadly game with Despero.

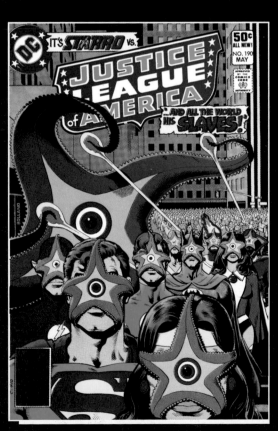

***JLA* (Vol. 1) #190 (May 1981)**
The Justice League learns Starro's
key weakness, but not before many
fall to the alien's powers.

THE SATELLITE

The Justice League made the decision to move to a location far from the prying eyes of its enemies. With funds from billionaire Bruce Wayne and technology borrowed from the Hawkmen of Thanagar, the team constructed a secret satellite that silently circled the Earth in geostationary orbit, 22,300 miles above Earth.

MEMBERS

Superman
Batman
Wonder Woman
The Flash
Green Lantern
Aquaman
Green Arrow
The Atom
Hawkman
Black Canary
Phantom Stranger
Elongated Man
Red Tornado
Hawkgirl
Zatanna
Firestorm

Changing of the guard
The League's roster changed significantly during the period in which they were based aboard the satellite. Both Batman and Martian Manhunter left the team for personal reasons, while Wonder Woman briefly stepped down when she lost her powers.

HOME AWAY FROM HOME

To keep the satellite accessible, the League built teleport platforms that could be used to transport to the orbiting headquarters. Outfitted with highly sensitive surveillance technology, the satellite monitor station could detect trouble anywhere in the solar system, and was manned at all times by rotating members of the super-team. As such, the satellite was built with an entire deck dedicated to private quarters for those who needed them.

ALIEN ASSAULT

The satellite base was eventually taken out of commission during a Martian attack. The wrecked shell of what had once been the pride of the Justice League was finally destroyed when Red Tornado's android body self-destructed after being sabotaged.

FEBRUARY 1971

MAIN CHARACTERS
Hawkman • Batman •
Superman • Zatanna •
The Flash • The Atom •
Green Lantern

SUPPORTING CHARACTERS
Silver Sorceress • Wandjina •
Blue Jay • Jack B. Quick

MAIN LOCATIONS
Earth • Cam-Nam-Lao

JUSTICE LEAGUE OF AMERICA (VOL.1) #87

THE LEAGUE MEETS A TEAM FROM A DISTANT WORLD— THE CHAMPIONS OF ANGOR!

When searching for the source of a sinister robotic probe, the Justice League finds themselves facing off against an alien super-team with startlingly familiar powers. These abilities both rival and mirror those of the Earth's greatest champions.

1 Upon encountering a mysterious robot, Batman and Hawkman are badly beaten. The powerful machine, calculating the probability of more superpowered heroes arriving on the scene, determines that it would be best served if it lures the world's champions out into the open. In this way, it can defeat them quicker.

2 Several members of the Justice League respond to the emergency signal the robot has used as a lure, only to discover that Batman and Hawkman have both been driven insane! The winged Thanagarian is now uncharacteristically fearful, while Batman declares himself king of the world, ordering the robot to attack the League.

3 Defeating the robot and sending Batman and Hawkman to the hospital, four members of the League trace the robot to a distant world—one ruined by a cataclysmic war. The team discovers that the robot was a drone, operating on the final orders of its long-lost makers. But before the heroes can leave, they are ambushed by another group of costumed beings.

"I'm king of the whole world!"

BATMAN

4 Unable to communicate with each other, the two teams very quickly find themselves engaged in battle. The newcomers are convinced that the Justice League is responsible for a robot that attacked their own world in the same manner as the events that occurred on Earth.

5 The battle is brutal. The Flash is challenged by the speedster Jack B. Quick. The Atom is paired against the shrinking hero Blue Jay. Green Lantern duels the weather-powered Wandjina, and Zatanna is locked in a mystic struggle with the Silver Sorceress.

6 When Zatanna and Green Lantern risk their own safety to heal the fallen Blue Jay, the alien heroes realize that the Justice League is peaceful. Both sides end the fighting. Parting as friends, the two super-teams return to their own worlds.

MAGIC AND MYSTERIES

With the move to an orbital satellite base and the world facing escalating levels of criminal activity—as well as increasingly dangerous cosmic threats—the Justice League expanded its roster once more. New heroes, young and old, were soon recruited to aid in the defense of the Earth and the galaxy.

"Firestorm...why don't you try to grow up? This isn't a movie."
— ELONGATED MAN

FIRESTORM

The original Firestorm was a fusion of two men: Professor Martin Stein and young Ronnie Raymond. The pair were caught in a nuclear accident that transformed them both into a single entity. The being was controlled by Ronnie, while Stein was relegated to a phantom presence only Ronnie could perceive. As Firestorm, the pair could use their powers to alter the molecular composition of almost anything. Ronnie relied on the experience and scientific background of the ghostly Stein to guide the physical actions of Firestorm. After Ronnie's "death," teenager Jason Rusch assumed the lead role in the Firestorm Matrix.

ZATANNA

Daughter of the stage magician Giovanni Zatara, Zatanna can cast a wide variety of magical spells by incanting words backward. As a teenager, she was friends with a young Bruce Wayne while he studied under her father during his training to become Batman. When her father went missing, Zatanna turned to members of the Justice League for help. She eventually became a member of the team, adding much needed magical insight and abilities to the roster. Her relationships within the team were later strained when it was revealed she used magic to help "rehabilitate" super-villains.

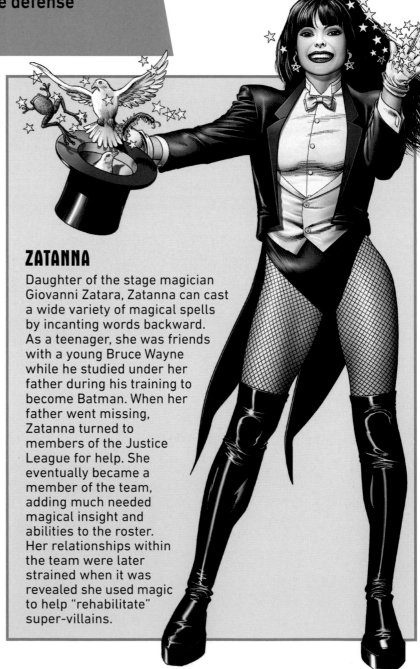

ELONGATED MAN

Obsessed with performers and contortionists as a child, Ralph Dibny became determined to find a scientific chemical that would enable him to twist his form in a similar manner. Eventually discovering an extract of a rare fruit called "gingo," Dibny was able to give himself astonishing stretching powers, and became the super-flexible hero named Elongated Man. A frequent partner of the Flash, Elongated Man went on to join the Justice League. As an amateur sleuth, Dibny often uses his powers for detective work, operating alongside his wife and longtime partner-in-crimebusting, Sue Dibny.

HAWKWOMAN

A Thanagarian police officer, Shayera Hol came to Earth with her husband Katar Hol, aka Hawkman, on the hunt for the shape-shifting villain Byth. Once the villain was captured and taken back to Thanagar for punishment, Shayera, along with her husband, returned to Earth, where she adopted the name Shiera Hall. Though she joined the Justice League some time after her husband, she became far more dedicated to the team in the long run.

RED TORNADO

Although his android body was constructed by the Justice League enemy T.O. Morrow, Red Tornado quickly abandoned the directives of his creator and chose to work alongside the heroes of Earth. Over the years, it became apparent that Morrow hadn't just built the Tornado; he had used its body to house a sentient entity known as the Tornado Champion, an elemental creature found on the planet Rann. Constantly working to become more human in behavior, Red Tornado eventually took on the role of mentor and trainer of Earth's younger heroes.

THE PHANTOM STRANGER

No one knows the true origins of the Phantom Stranger. Many believe he is an ancient being, cursed to walk the world after questioning the powers that lie beyond the grave. Others think he was an angel who refused to choose a side in the wars between Heaven and Hell. Some even believe he is a man trapped in a time loop, who sacrificed his existence to stop an avatar of Anti-Life. Though the Stranger was technically a member of the Justice League, many of his teammates cannot clearly remember if the Phantom ever actually fought by their side.

NO MAN ESCAPES THE MANHUNTERS!

When an ancient enemy of the Oan Guardians of the galaxy enacts a sinister plan for revenge, entire worlds risk destruction. Only the Justice League can uncover the truth, as they face an entire legion of mighty warriors—a group claiming to be working to save lives and protect the galaxy from terror.

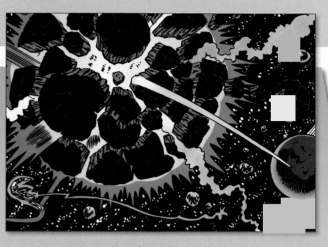

Justice League of America (Vol. 1) #140 (Mar. 1977)
In trying to save Orinda by demolishing its moon, Green Lantern unwittingly ended up destroying the planet. Or so he believed...

AN OVERWHELMING FORCE

Having called an emergency meeting of the Justice League of America at the Wayne Foundation, Green Lantern is attacked by a Manhunter. This fearsome masked figure is powerful enough to take down Green Arrow and Black Canary in a matter of seconds. Only Green Lantern has the power to face this threat, but instead of fighting the strange foe, he willingly surrenders as a prisoner.

GUILTY CONSCIENCE

Imprisoned by the Manhunters, Green Lantern is brought before the Grandmaster of this sect of soldiers. The Emerald Warrior confesses that he accidentally blew up a planet while trying to save it—the world of Orinda. When it was obliterated, millions of lives were lost. As a result, the Manhunters—galactic bounty hunters—have arrested Green Lantern, and intend to hold him responsible for his crimes.

Justice League of America (Vol. 1) #140 (Mar. 1977)
After their investigations lead them to a red moon, the Justice League is confronted by a gigantic Magnosaurus.

Justice League of America (Vol. 1) #140 (Mar. 1977)
Smashing through a door, the Manhunter declares he has come for Green Lantern.

> *"All of this is lies!!"*
> **SUPERMAN**

Justice League of America (Vol. 1) **#141 (Apr. 1977)**
The Manhunters are revealed to be androids, built by the Guardians.

INVISIBLE ORBIT

While investigating the incident, the JLA is attacked by an ancient monster on another moon of the supposedly destroyed Orinda. During a battle with the beast, Batman realizes if the moon is still in orbit, the planet must still exist. Even more sinisterly, it appears that the Manhunters are not just a peace-keeping force, but are set to launch galactic war.

RAGE OF THE MACHINE

The Guardians of Oa finally reveal the truth—that they had constructed the Manhunters, who were in reality powerful androids. They were built long before the creation of the Green Lantern Corps and programmed to police the galaxy. However, after the Manhunters concluded that they were superior to their masters, they rebelled against the Guardians. Since that time, the outcast machines have disguised themselves, while working slowly toward the moment where they could enact their revenge.

Justice League of America (Vol. 1) **#141 (Apr. 1977)**
The Manhunters' human agent, Mark Shaw, turns on the Grandmaster, as he learns of the android nature of the warriors.

MECHANICAL MASTERS

Realizing that they have been deceived, the Justice League turns the tables on the Manhunters. They reveal to the galaxy that the supposed destruction of the planet Orinda was part of a plot to discredit the Guardians and disband the Green Lantern Corps. In the process, they also expose the mechanical nature of the Manhunters, leading one human agent of the vengeful androids—Mark Shaw—to turn against his former masters.

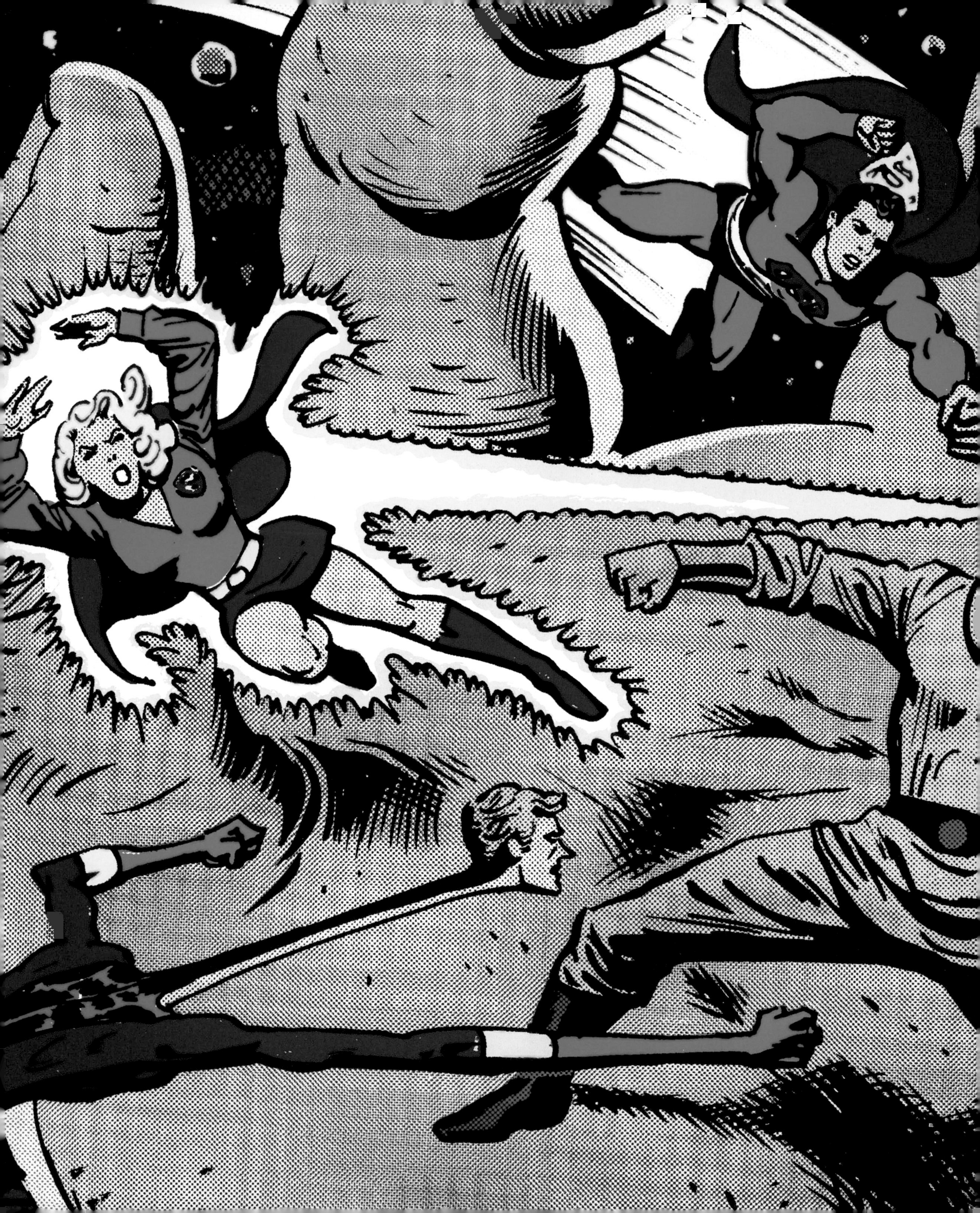

Justice League of America (Vol. 1) #134 (Sep. 1976)
Tricked into combat by an advanced race called the Krill, the Justice League and the alien tyrant Despero find themselves engaged in a savage battle. It is one that neither side can truly win—unless they change the rules.

JULY 1977

MAIN CHARACTERS
Green Arrow • Wonder Woman • Aquaman • The Flash • Martian Manhunter • Batman • Superman

SUPPORTING CHARACTERS
Robin • Hal Jordan • Vigilante • Blackhawks • Plastic Man • Congo Bill • Congorilla • Adam Strange • Robotman • Challengers of the Unknown • Lois Lane • Jimmy Olsen • Rip Hunter

MAIN LOCATIONS
JLA satellite • Middletown • Metropolis

JUSTICE LEAGUE OF AMERICA (VOL.1) #144

GREEN ARROW UNCOVERS THE TRUE ORIGIN OF THE JUSTICE LEAGUE.

For years, the founding members of the Justice League claimed that they came together as a team in response to an Appellaxian invasion. However, after digging through files stored on the JLA's satellite, Green Arrow discovers another version of events leading to the League's formation—a story he has never heard.

1 Upon discovering files in the Justice League computer archive that contradict the team's origin he has always been told, Green Arrow demands answers from his teammates. In response, Superman and Green Lantern activate a pre-recorded message from the Martian Manhunter.

2 Retelling the tale of his arrival on Earth, J'onn J'onzz explains how his first interactions with the human populace revealed small-minded bigotry and paranoid prejudice. He quickly chose to hide his identity out of fear of persecution. For four years he stayed hidden—until...

3 J'onn discovers that his attempts to contact his homeworld have been received by an old archnemesis of his—the White Martian warlord, Commander Blanx. Unable to defeat the villain on his own, J'onn briefly encounters The Flash—his first meeting with a costumed hero.

4 The appearance of Commander Blanx and the White Martians starts a chain reaction of fear—one that the heroes of Earth assemble to counter. Forming multiple teams to combat this apparent Martian invasion, the heroes split off to counter the attacks.

"Gosh! But aren't you a Martian too?"

ROBIN

5 While Superman, Aquaman, Wonder Woman, and The Flash battle the Martians, Batman and Robin rescue the Martians' prisoner, J'onn J'onnz. After J'onn shares his secret weakness with his rescuers—his vulnerability to fire—the newly formed team combines its efforts to repel the invading army of White Martians.

6 Deciding to protect the Martian Manhunter's secret, the group forms an official team—a league dedicated to upholding justice. To help the Earth accept their alien teammate, they introduce J'onn to the world during the Appellaxian invasion, claiming that adventure as their "first" meeting.

CRISIS ON NEW GENESIS

The Justice League of America and the Justice Society of America face their greatest challenge to date, when they unite in battle against the newly reborn Darkseid and the legions of Apokolips.

BRAVE NEW WORLD

The JLA and the JSA, having now turned their meetings into annual events, find their plans for a party derailed when members of both teams are hijacked and dropped into a strange world—New Genesis, home of the New Gods. Only Superman has ever ventured to this distant, other-dimensional place. Before the teams can get their bearing, Firestorm flies off to explore—heedless of the risks.

Justice League of America (Vol. 1) #183 (Oct. 1980)
The JLA and JSA are astonished to find themselves on New Genesis.

A PLEA FOR HELP

After a brief altercation with Orion, the being known as Metron reveals himself. It was he who brought the teams to New Genesis, seeking their help. During discussions, Big Barda and Mister Miracle explain that the entire population of New Genesis has been enslaved by the people of Apokolips, the evil mirror image world of New Genesis. Even worse, that malignant planet has formed a new alliance—with the Injustice Society.

Justice League of America (Vol. 1) #183 (Oct. 1980)
Metron welcomes the two teams to New Genesis— and begs their assistance.

Justice League of America (Vol. 1) #184 (Nov. 1980)
Mister Miracle outlines Darkseid's nightmarish plan to Huntress and Batman: to transport Apokolips to Earth-2's universe, destroying the JSA's homeworld.

POWER SHIFT

It soon becomes clear that the newly resurrected Darkseid seeks more than to live again. He intends to transport his world into the dimensional plane of Earth-2—home of the Justice Society. In the process, he will destroy all life on that world. Mistakenly, Darkseid believes that if he can relocate his world he can escape his past and the forces that continue to thwart him—the ancient Old Gods and his accursed brethren, the New Gods.

Justice League of America (Vol. 1) #183 (Oct. 1980)
On Apokolips, Power Girl, Orion, and Firestorm learn the truth: the dreaded Lord Darkseid has been resurrected!

RETURN OF EVIL

The united forces of three worlds assault Apokolips, discovering in the process the true reason for the abductions—to resurrect Darkseid, the most powerful villain that ever existed. Several of the heroes attempt to interrupt the procedure, but are overwhelmed by the forces of the Injustice Society. Before long, the Lord of Apokolips is restored to unholy existence. Meanwhile, the rest of the heroes seek out the imprisoned people of New Genesis.

"Somehow they've brought him back from death!"

ORION

Justice League of America (Vol. 1) #185 (Dec. 1980)
Darkseid is blasted from the cosmos, as the beam from his re-creation machine strikes him instead of its intended target.

FALL OF A TITAN

The heroes storm the imperial palace of Apokolips with an army of freed citizens of New Genesis, managing to turn Darkseid's Omega Beams back on him. Refusing defeat, Darkseid activates the re-creation machine that resurrected him, planning on completing his mission of moving Apokolips. However, unbeknownst to the Lord of Apokolips, Metron has recalibrated the targeting system, directing it to strike Darkseid instead, disintegrating his body.

The era of self-appointed intergalactic protectors was coming to an end. The world's problems were proving much too demanding for a Justice League distracted by the non-stop perils from space. The team was undergoing the first of several upheavals, and would never quite be the same.

DOWN TO EARTH

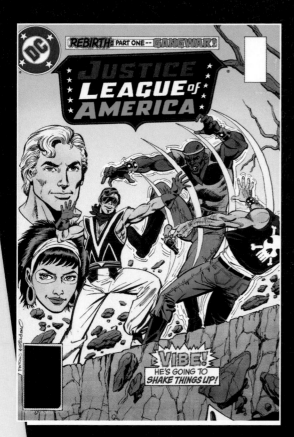

JLA (Vol. 1) #233 (Dec. 1984)
Looking to expand its roster, the Justice League
recruits a former gang member turned hero.

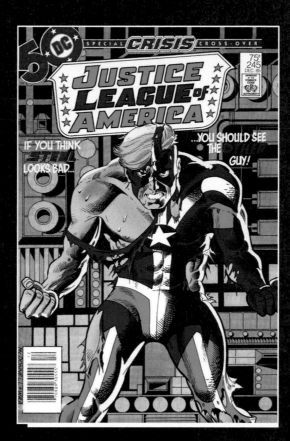

JLA (Vol. 1) #245 (Dec. 1985)
Steel must defeat his insane grandfather, the
World War II hero called Commander Steel.

JLA (Vol. 1) #249 (Apr. 1986)
An alien being living in the old League
headquarters awakens, draining
the life force of the heroes.

JLA (Vol. 1) #258 (Jan. 1987)
After facing the titanic creature Brimstone,
the team is ambushed by Amazo,
Professor Ivo's avenging android.

THE BUNKER

After Aquaman invoked his right as a founding member to disband the League, he reformed the team with new members. In need of a new headquarters, the group was approached by the hero Steel, who offered the specially built Bunker in exchange for a spot on the new team.

MEMBERS

Martian Manhunter

Aquaman

Zatanna

Elongated Man

Steel

Vixen

Vibe

Gypsy

Batman

Taking charge
Not long after forming a new version of the Justice League, Aquaman succumbed to the growing pressures of his private life and left the Martian Manhunter in charge of the reconstituted team.

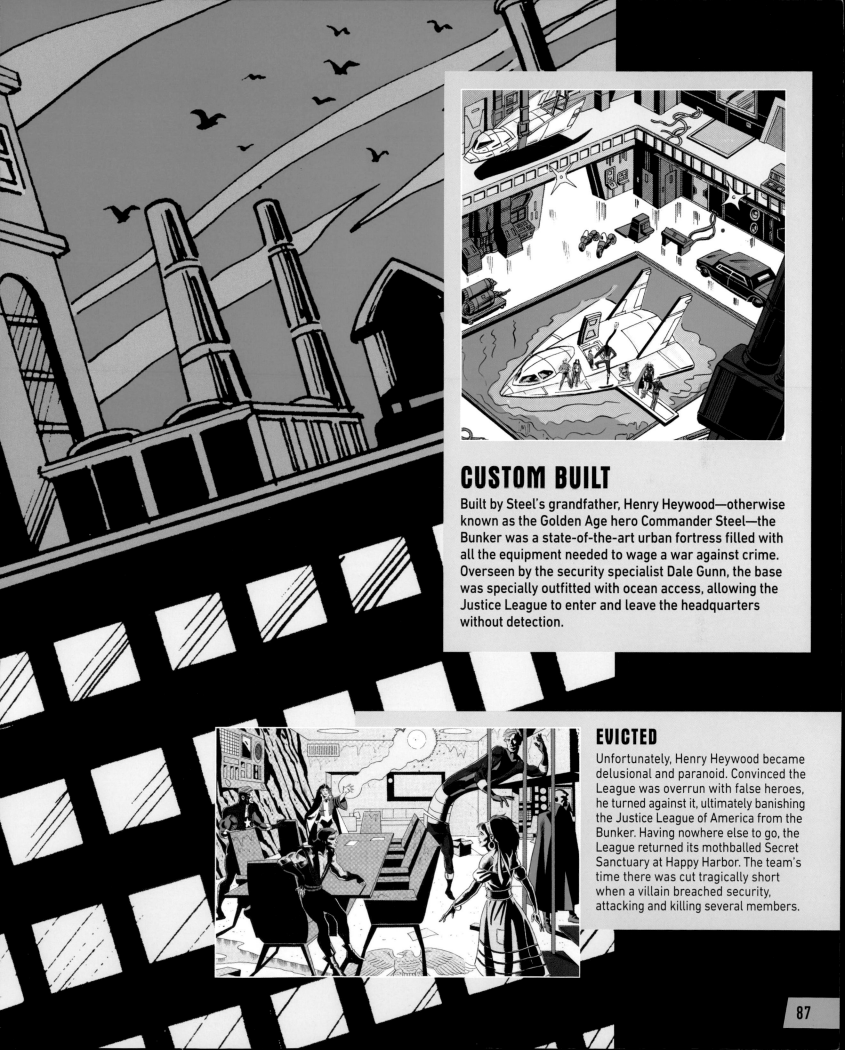

CUSTOM BUILT

Built by Steel's grandfather, Henry Heywood—otherwise known as the Golden Age hero Commander Steel—the Bunker was a state-of-the-art urban fortress filled with all the equipment needed to wage a war against crime. Overseen by the security specialist Dale Gunn, the base was specially outfitted with ocean access, allowing the Justice League to enter and leave the headquarters without detection.

EVICTED

Unfortunately, Henry Heywood became delusional and paranoid. Convinced the League was overrun with false heroes, he turned against it, ultimately banishing the Justice League of America from the Bunker. Having nowhere else to go, the League returned its mothballed Secret Sanctuary at Happy Harbor. The team's time there was cut tragically short when a villain breached security, attacking and killing several members.

STREET FIGHTERS

With most of the Justice League's founding members out of the team, Aquaman sought out new heroes with a resolute commitment to the cause of justice. These new recruits were found fighting common criminals on the street, rather than disappearing for weeks at a time into alternate dimensions.

> "The Justice League has put itself on the line to **save** you all— **over** and over again. We've **bled** for you!"
>
> STEEL

GYPSY

A juvenile runaway from the suburbs, Gypsy was one of the youngest heroes to ever serve in the League, joining when she was just 14. Her illusion-casting and chameleon-like powers allowed her to infiltrate almost any location, while also letting her fight without being seen. She also possessed precognitive abilities that she had difficulty controlling. Unfortunately, she was unable to save her family from the wrath of Despero, a loss that haunts her to this day. Though her time in the League was brief, she formed a strong bond with the Martian Manhunter, and the two remained close long after the Detroit incarnation of the Justice League of America came to an end.

STEEL

Grandson of the World War II hero Commander Steel, Hank Heywood unwillingly underwent a series of operations to transform him into a Super Hero like his grandfather. Unknown to Hank, the operations were needed to save his life. The young man was all too aware that the original Commander Steel had in all likelihood been driven mad by his own metal implants, and could never quite forgive the painful and cruel treatment he himself had received. While Steel was a member of the JLA, the team resided in a bunker in Detroit provided by the original Commander, who sought to live vicariously through his grandson.

VIXEN

Descended from a legendary warrior named Tantu, Mari McCabe grew up in a village in Africa. After her father was murdered by her uncle, Mari claimed the Tantu Totem as her own. As she had only ever wanted to use the power to protect others, the artifact granted Mari the abilities of any animal on Earth. Using these, she entered the wider world as a hero, initially fighting poachers and terrorists. Eventually, she found herself a home in the Justice League, joining several other recent recruits as the new faces of the well-established team. After Despero destroyed the JLA, Mari decided to travel with the similarly powered Animal Man, helping him gain control over his fading abilities. Later, she joined Amanda Waller's Suicide Squad, hoping her time in the team would help her control her increased savagery.

VIBE

Paco Ramone was a street gang member who decided to use his metahuman powers to be a Super Hero after he discovered the Justice League was setting up operations in Detroit. An angry young man with a chip on his shoulder, Paco took the name Vibe and was responsible for much of the friction within the new incarnation of the team. Despite this, his unique seismic vibrational powers added a much-needed edge to the roster and he soon became a fixture. Vibe was tragically killed battling Amazo. His body has since been resurrected and put to evil use on more than one occasion by super-villains. After his death, his younger brother became the hero Reverb and joined Gypsy in the Conglomerate, a corporate-sponsored team briefly led by Booster Gold.

DESPERO... REBORN

An old enemy of the Justice League returns from the depths of the past seeking revenge. Despero, tyrant of the distant world Kalanor, lost everything when he sought to use the JLA as pawns in his bid to control his homeworld. Still tormented by his defeat, he subjected himself to the mutating nuclear Flame of Py'tar. Now it appears nothing can stop him.

AN ENEMY RETURNS

While Batman attempts to train the new Justice League, several of his teammates go about their personal lives or have solo adventures. Unbeknown to them all, a rage-filled force is hurtling toward them at great speed: Despero, mutated and energized through a tortuous ordeal in nuclear fire. This sworn enemy of the League has only one thought in his mind: vengeance.

Justice League of America (Vol. 1) #251 (Jun. 1986)
On his mission of revenge, Despero will let nothing stand in the way of his destroying the Justice League.

Justice League of America (Vol. 1) #251 (Jun. 1986)
Landing on the Justice League's shattered satellite, Despero is enraged when he discovers that the League is not present.

RUINS OF THE PAST

Arriving at the abandoned wreckage of the Justice League satellite, Despero seeks clues to the whereabouts of his foes. It does not take him long to conclude that the team can only be in one place: the surface of the world they have sought so long to protect. Using his eye-beam to destroy the remains of the satellite around him, Despero feels the ruined outpost fall into the gravitational field of the Earth. Rather than flee, he rides it down, letting the burning fires of reentry fuel his hatred.

> *"Hiding isn't the only trick I know..."*
> GYPSY

***Justice League of America* (Vol. 1) #254 (Sep. 1986)**
Reeling from Gypsy's telepathic attack, Despero succumbs to panic as the solar energy begins to sear his skin.

ON THE HUNT

Crashing to Earth, Despero begins slaughtering his way through the population, demanding the Justice League makes itself known. Telepathically tearing thoughts from his victims' minds, he learns that a new Justice League has been formed. Deciding to draw his enemies out, the alien sets his sights on Gotham City, recalling it to be the home of Batman. Once there, it doesn't take long for Despero to unleash chaos and devastation.

***Justice League of America* (Vol. 1) #252 (Jul. 1986)**
Emerging from the burning wreckage of the JLA satellite on Earth, Despero learns a new League has formed.

MENTAL MIGHT

As Despero revels in his new powers of matter manipulation, Batman figures out the truth. Despero needs to continually recharge himself within nuclear fire or he will die. As several members of the League attempt to distract Despero so that the flame he has created can be destroyed, the unassuming Gypsy fires her own considerable telepathic power at the monster. In response, Despero instinctively unleashes all his energy in a flailing attempt to defend himself from her assault.

AN ENEMY DESTROYED

Vibe takes advantage of the moment and uses his power to extinguish the energy source, cutting off an already weakened Despero. The effect is instantaneous, as the alien invader's body immediately consumes itself in a spectacular implosion of energy. With Despero gone, the effects of his power disappear, and Gotham City returns to normal, leaving a wounded and exhausted, but triumphant Justice League to return to its headquarters.

***Justice League of America* (Vol. 1) #254 (Sep. 1986)**
The JLA narrowly escapes near death as Despero violently implodes.

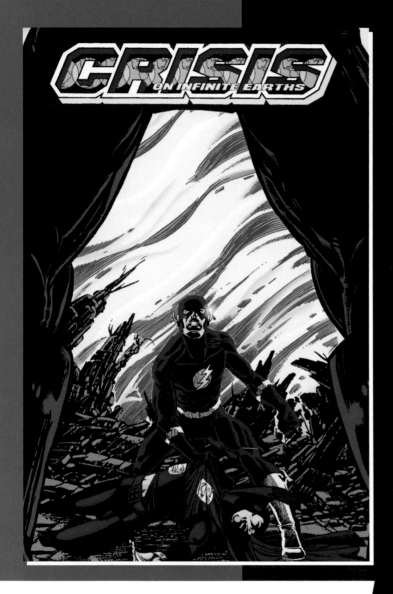

CRISIS ON INFINITE EARTHS (VOL.1) #8

THE FLASH RUNS HIS FINAL RACE IN AN EFFORT TO SAVE THE MULTIVERSE.

Across the multiverse, a wave of antimatter energy has been consuming realities in a single heartbeat. This is the work of the Anti-Monitor as he seeks to conquer all creation. As a precaution, this enemy of life has imprisoned one of the most dangerous heroes, The Flash, whose dimension-traversing powers put the villain's plans at risk.

NOVEMBER 1985

MAIN CHARACTERS
The Flash • Anti-Monitor •
Psycho Pirate

SUPPORTING CHARACTERS
Qwardians

MAIN LOCATIONS
The Antimatter Universe
of Qward

1 As the Anti-Monitor burns his way through the multiverse, The Flash finds himself a prisoner on the planet Qward. Seeing an opportunity to strike back at the enormous evil that is threatening to consume his Earth, The Flash slowly increases his internal vibrations until he can escape his bonds.

2 The Flash first takes down his primary tormentor, the Psycho Pirate—a low-level villain whose emotion-manipulating powers have been enhanced by the Anti-Monitor. Overcoming feelings of fear and humiliation that have been induced in him, The Flash devises a plan to strike at his true captor.

3 Hurtling through Qward at super-speed, The Flash forces Psycho Pirate to use his powers on the emotions of the Weaponers of Qward. These lightning-hurling shock troops are manipulated into turning against their master, the Anti-Monitor, thus keeping the villain distracted.

4 With the Psycho Pirate knocked unconscious and the Anti-Monitor occupied, The Flash vibrates his way through the hull of the Anti-Monitor's reality-erasing cannon, a terrifying weapon that harnesses concentrated antimatter. Realizing that there is only one way to destabilize the energy, The Flash begins to run as fast as he can in a circle around the accumulated power.

"There's hope... There is always hope..."

THE FLASH

5 The energy from the weapon is draining, but in the process The Flash's life force is being torn from him. Little by little, he is dying, yet still he runs faster. As he runs, a window through time opens up in front of him. He sees past allies and enemies, including his sidekick, Kid Flash, calling out to him. Though others can see The Flash as well, they cannot reach the hero.

6 In his last moments, The Flash sends messages back through these windows of time—warnings, words of hope, and pleas for help. After he causes the Anti-Monitor's cannon to explode, all that remains of The Flash is an empty costume and the lightning bolt ring he once wore so proudly.

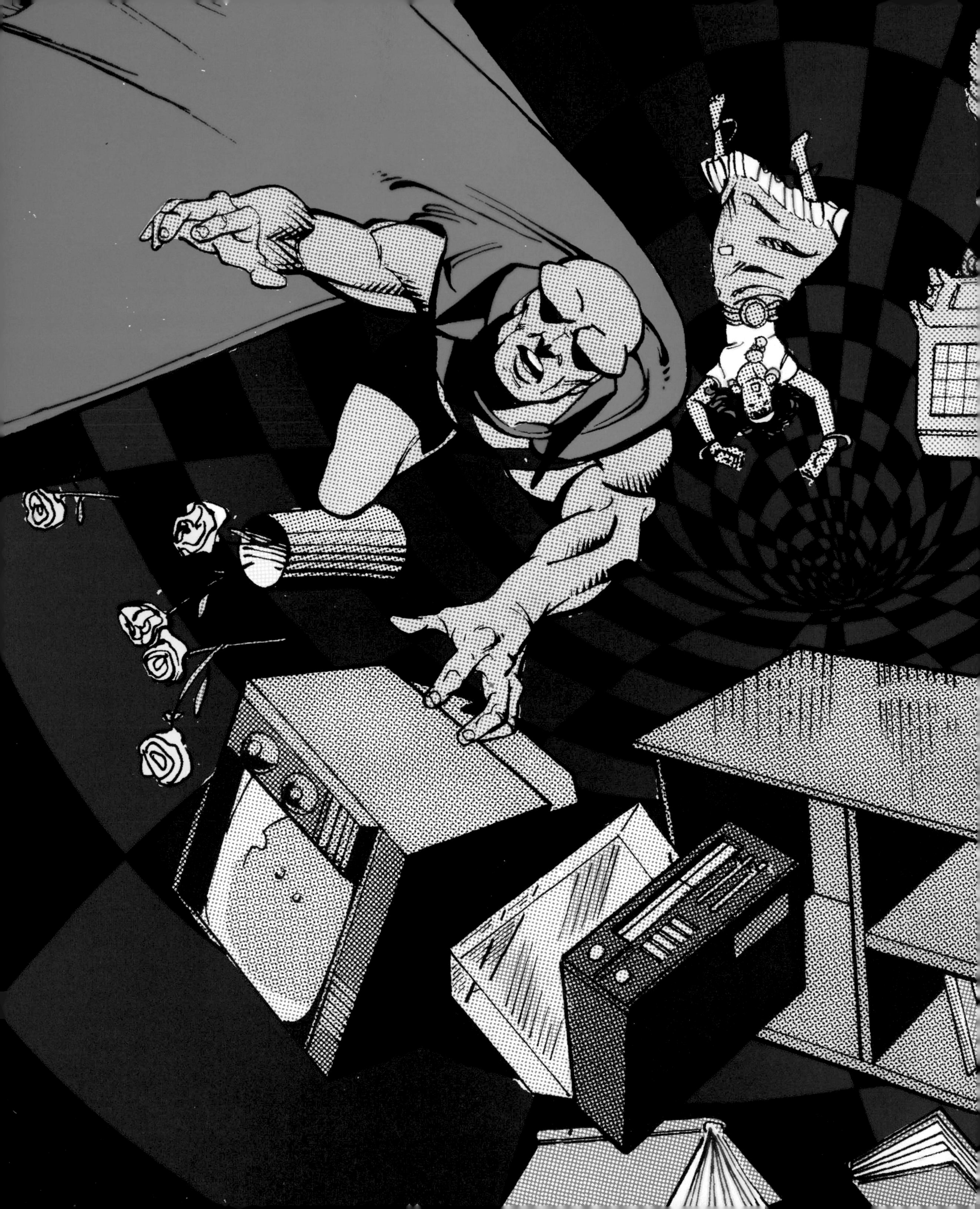

Justice League of America (Vol. 1)
#257 (Dec. 1986)
Trapped in the mind of an enemy, the
Justice League of America must navigate
an increasingly insane pseudo-reality. This
realm was created by a power far beyond
the reach of mere mortals—one strangely
interested in Zatanna and her abilities.

MINDGAMES!

A TRAGIC ENDING

After a modest series of adventures, the Justice League originally formed by Aquaman is still struggling to find its place in a world that sees them as an inferior replacement team. At this time, when the Earth seems least ready to defend itself, the forces of evil emerge from the darkness to strike their deadliest blow...

> *"Who among you will be the first to lend his heart, his mind, his soul...?"*
>
> GLORIOUS GODFREY

REPUTATION MATTERS

Concluding that the planet Earth would become easier to subjugate if humanity lost faith in its heroes, Darkseid enacts a new, elaborate plan of conquest. His first step is to create a titanic creature of rage and fire in the heart of a fusion generator— a being called Brimstone. Elsewhere, another massive villain attacks, this one calling itself Macro-Man.

Legends (Vol. 1) #2 (Dec. 1986)
Brimstone declares his intention to purge Earth of "false gods."

Legends (Vol. 1) #1 (Nov. 1986)
Darkseid decides to strike at the core of Earth's heroes by destroying the very concept of legends.

Legends (Vol. 1) #4 (Feb. 1987)
As G. Gordon Godfrey, Glorious
Godfrey holds an anti-hero
rally in Gotham City.

Legends (Vol. 1) #3 (Jan. 1987)
Enchantress, Captain Boomerang, and Blockbuster are conscripted by Waller.

A SUICIDAL SQUAD

Unconvinced that the world's heroes are up to the task of defeating the threats Earth now faces, US government agent Amanda Waller enlists Rick Flagg to reactivate Task Force X. In the past, this secret team was sent into deadly scenarios and became known as the "Suicide Squad." Meanwhile, in his efforts to defeat Macro-Man, Captain Marvel seemingly burns the villain alive with his magic lightning. In truth, this apparent murder is a ruse by Darkseid to discredit the heroes.

MOB RULES

Darkseid's main agent on Earth, Glorious Godfrey, continues to stir up anti-Super Hero sentiment by posing as an extremist politician with an agenda to overthrow the government.
Manipulating those citizens who find fear and rage too tempting to resist, the persuasive villain outfits volunteers with cybernetic dog-like vehicles called Warhounds. These sinister machines of Apokolips are designed to spread terror and empower humanity against superhumans— all the while further subverting them to Darkseid's will.

Justice League of America (Vol. 1) #258 (Jan. 1987)
Professor Ivo's android walks away, leaving Justice League member Vibe lying dead in the street.

Legends (Vol. 1) #5
(Mar. 1987)
Gathered together by Doctor Fate, the heroes confront Glorious Godfrey in Metropolis.

HEROIC TO THE LAST

Failing to stop Brimstone themselves, the Justice League returns to its headquarters feeling defeated. Taking advantage of their distraction, Professor Ivo launches an attack with his android Amazo. Vibe and Steel are killed, while Gypsy barely escapes with her life. The remaining members of the team are shaken by their losses, and the Justice League is soon disbanded.

YOUTH IN REVOLT

The heroes strike back against Godfrey, uniting after Doctor Fate seeks them out. Before long they are able to dismantle the Warhounds, but Godfrey's influence over the public remains. Only one group of the civilian population is uncorrupted by the villain's hate and fear: the children. As the youngest citizens rush forward to protect their heroes from the mob, Godfrey grows frustrated and lashes out, hitting a child. The act of violence breaks his spell and the people turn against him, ending Darkseid's bid for control of Earth.

THE EMBASSIES

With the League reinvented as an independent branch of the U.N., business tycoon Max Lord set himself up as the chief of operations of an international hero franchise. Under his direction, the Justice League International became a peacekeeping force, with headquarters scattered across the globe, and built and staffed by local governments.

MEMBERS

Europe

Captain Atom

Rocket Red 4

Animal Man

Wonder Woman

Power Girl

The Flash
(Wally West)

Elongated Man

Metamorpho

Crimson Fox

Silver Sorceress

Blue Jay

America

Batman

Martian Manhunter

Blue Beetle

Black Canary

Captain Marvel

Doctor Fate

Mister Miracle

Green Lantern
(Guy Gardner)

Booster Gold

Captain Atom

Rocket Red 4

Fire

Ice

Staff

Maxwell Lord

Oberon

L-Ron

Kilowog

Catherine Cobert

Sue Dibny

Michael and
Lisa Morice

Esteban Sanchez

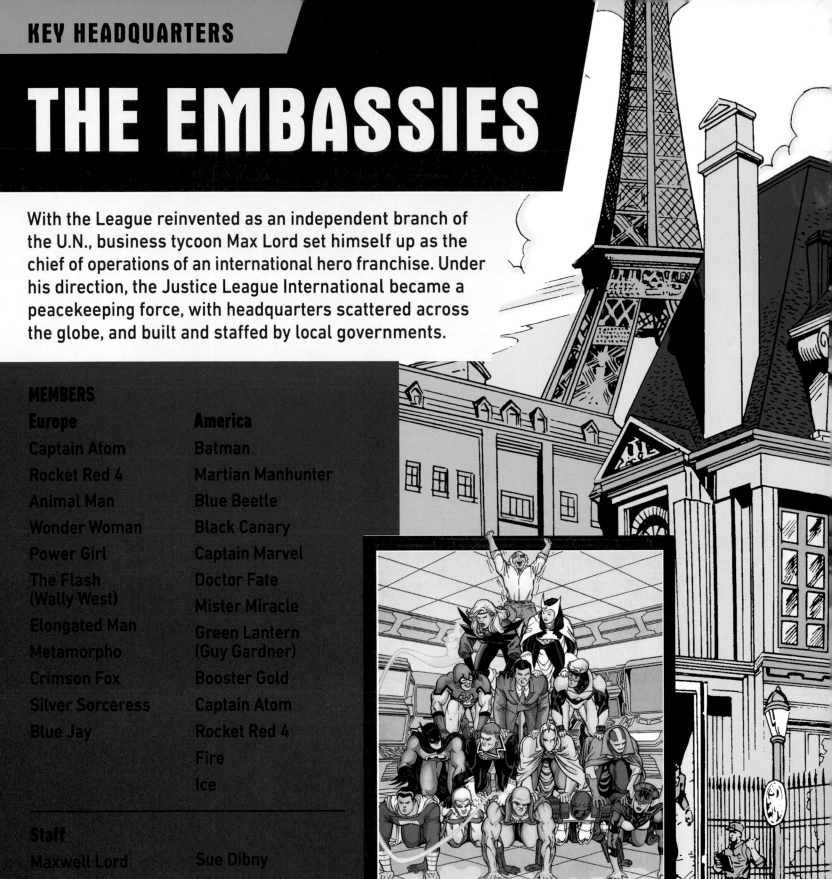

Heroes for hire
Originally led by Batman, the membership of the embassy era's Justice League was constantly shifting, depending on the availability of heroes and the requirements of the mission.

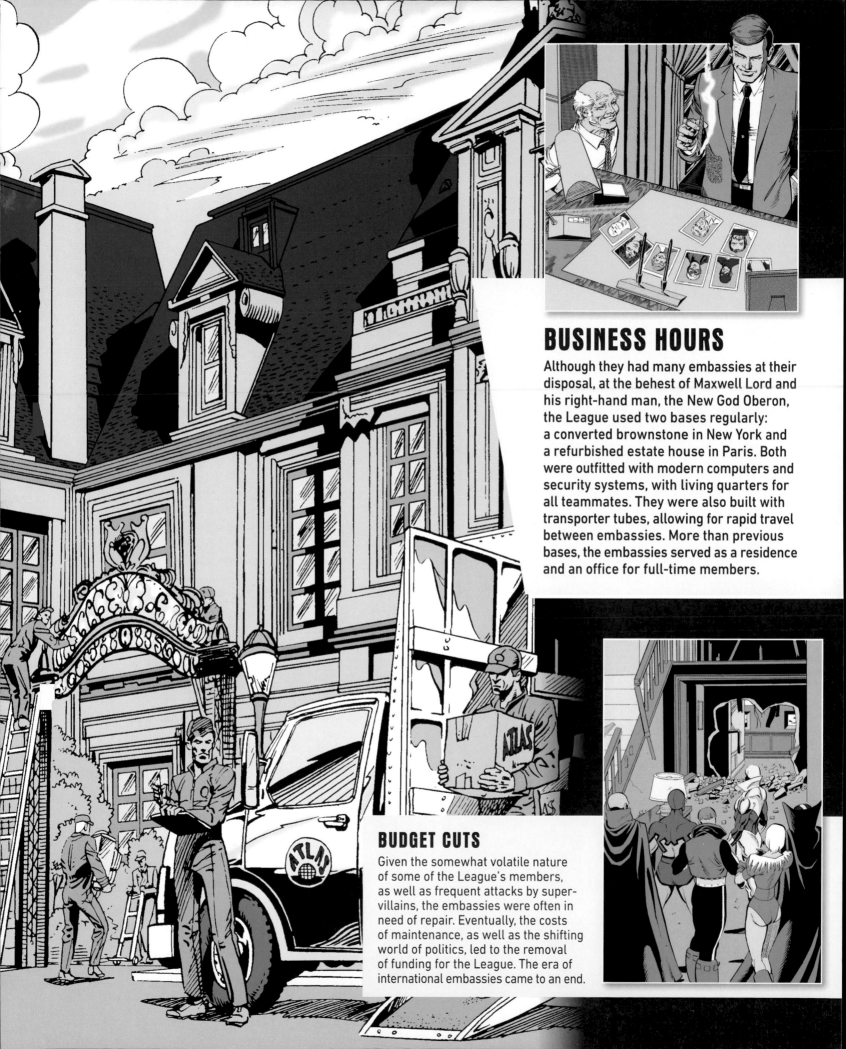

BUSINESS HOURS

Although they had many embassies at their
disposal, at the behest of Maxwell Lord and
his right-hand man, the New God Oberon,
the League used two bases regularly:
a converted brownstone in New York and
a refurbished estate house in Paris. Both
were outfitted with modern computers and
security systems, with living quarters for
all teammates. They were also built with
transporter tubes, allowing for rapid travel
between embassies. More than previous
bases, the embassies served as a residence
and an office for full-time members.

BUDGET CUTS

Given the somewhat volatile nature
of some of the League's members,
as well as frequent attacks by super-
villains, the embassies were often in
need of repair. Eventually, the costs
of maintenance, as well as the shifting
world of politics, led to the removal
of funding for the League. The era of
international embassies came to an end.

A NEW BEGINNING

In the wake of the carnage unleashed by Professor Ivo on the Justice League in Detroit and the widespread anti-Super Hero atmosphere generated by Darkseid's servant, Glorious Godfrey, several heroes band together to try and form a new team. This Justice League is soon plagued by familiar villains, new foes, and the most frustrating enemy it could ever face: itself.

***Justice League* (Vol. 1) #2 (Jun. 1987)**
The Champions of Angor reveal themselves and their intent to destroy Bialya's nuclear missiles.

SUPER PROFESSIONAL

Gathering together in the old Justice League headquarters in Happy Harbor, the new League quickly attempts to settle into their new home and get down to business. However, this effort is derailed within minutes as a no-holds-barred brawl breaks out—largely centered around the most arrogant Green Lantern to ever wear a power ring, Guy Gardner. Arriving in the middle of the chaos, Batman assumes the role of team leader and decisively takes control, intimidating the rest of the group into behaving themselves.

***Justice League* (Vol. 1) #1 (May 1987)**
Guy Gardner blasts Captain Marvel at the inaugural meeting of the new League.

COMPLETELY DISARMING

It soon becomes clear that someone is manipulating the League, inviting in new members and pushing the team into dangerous situations—in full view of the media—without warning. Unfortunately, before the team can investigate further, they discover that three members of the alien Champions of Angor are present in the nation of Bialya. These Champions create an international incident by dismantling the country's nuclear weapons.

***Justice League* (Vol. 1) #3 (Jul. 1987)**
The League is taken aback as Max Lord introduces new team member Booster Gold.

UNINVITED GUESTS

Barely avoiding starting a war with Russia, the Justice League defuses the situation—though not before the hero of Angor called Wandjina is critically injured, halting the mysteriously timed meltdown of a Russian power plant. Returning to America, the League is alarmed to find visitors in their supposedly secret headquarters: entrepreneur Maxwell Lord and hero Booster Gold.

Justice League (Vol. 1) #7 (Nov. 1987)
The brand new Justice League International is introduced to the world at the United Nations building.

> *"Batman belted him—and I missed it?"*
>
> **BLACK CANARY**

ANOTHER EVIL SATELLITE

Maxwell Lord manages to convince the Justice League to accept Booster as a member after the hero prevents a surprise attack by the Royal Flush Gang. However, Batman is suspicious of Lord and the recent coincidences. Public opinion is swaying in the League's favor—until a media firebrand called Jack Ryder begins attacking the team's credibility. In response to this shift in opinion, a strange satellite activates and unleashes a deadly laser beam, targeting several American nuclear bases—and only the Justice League can stop it in time.

Justice League (Vol. 1) #4 (Aug. 1987)
Booster Gold proves his worth by holding his own against the entire Royal Flush Gang.

UNEXPECTED BONUS

The Justice League attempts to disable the rogue satellite. In the process the team learns that the machine is rigged to both avoid harming them and to film and broadcast the heroic action. Defusing the threat, the League returns to Earth to find that they have been embraced as the defenders of the world, and are being granted special consideration by the UN. In time, the League will discover that the evil artificial intelligence the Construct is behind everything, but for now they are in the position they need to be to save lives on an international level.

JUSTICE LEAGUE EUROPE

Justice League Europe was the European branch of the Justice League International, one of a few expansions of the heroic 'franchise'. Originally, the League were magnificently stationed at the embassy in Paris, before being forced to operate from England after losing UN funding.

CRIMSON FOX

Crimson Fox was secretly two twin sisters, Vivian and Constance D'Aramis, whose pheromone powers could affect others' emotions and who were skilled in acrobatics and martial arts. Sadly, both sisters were killed in the line of duty fighting criminals.

ELONGATED MAN

Forever pursuing a life of adventure and mystery, Ralph Dibny and his wife, Sue, joined Justice League Europe. Although Ralph, as Elongated Man, used his stretching powers to fight crime on the frontline, it was often Sue, working tirelessly behind the scenes to organize the League, who was the real hero.

CAPTAIN ATOM

Nathaniel Adam was fused with an alien metal when exposed to a nuclear explosion. Instead of destroying him, the blast propelled the air force captain decades into the future, where he became the silver-skinned, quantum-powered hero Captain Atom.

ANIMAL MAN

Buddy Baker's amazing power to emulate the natural skills and strengths of animals quickly earned him a place in the European Justice League. It was a position Buddy, as Animal Man, wasn't sure he wanted, and he resigned not long after becoming a member.

CATHERINE COBERT

Head of the French Embassy and UN liaison to the Justice League of Europe, Catherine Cobert was competent, ambitious, compassionate—and wholly overqualified to be working with the JLE.

METAMORPHO

Rex Mason was an adventurer hired by unscrupulous businessman Simon Stagg to retrieve an artifact in Egypt. When Stagg learned of Rex's secret romance with his daughter Sapphire, he arranged for Rex to be killed and left for dead near a radioactive meteorite. However, the rock mutated Rex's body, giving him amazing elemental powers that he put to good use as the hero Metamorpho.

THE FLASH (WALLY WEST)

The second Flash to join the League, Wally West left the Teen Titans to assume the role of his beloved mentor, Barry Allen, after Barry seemingly sacrificed his life to defeat the Anti-Monitor. Wally joined the JLE to prove to the world that The Flash lived on.

WONDER WOMAN

After the Anti-Monitor attacked the Multiverse, Wonder Woman was struck with an energy blast that erased her history. Recreated by the gods, Wonder Woman was born again, and in this new incarnation joined the Justice League for the very first time.

SILVER SORCERESS

A member of the otherworldly Champions of Angor, Silver Sorceress joined the Justice League Europe after villains from her ruined world attacked Earth. Later, she died at the hands of her old foe, Dreamslayer.

BLUE JAY

A former Champion of Angor, Blue Jay followed his friend Silver Sorceress into the JLE. The flying, size-altering crimefighter remained active in the team for some time after the death of the Silver Sorceress, eventually leaving to find a planet he could feel more at home on than Earth.

POWER GIRL

A woman with an uncertain past, Kara Zor-L, aka Powergirl, is the Earth-2 counterpart of Supergirl. A former JSA member, the Kryptonian became trapped on Earth-1, where she joined the JLE. While Kara's understanding of her history has shifted many times, her heroic impulse remains steadfast.

DOOMSDAY

Possibly the deadliest foe the Man of Steel has ever faced, the marauding creature known as Doomsday is a near-immortal machine of hatred, born and bred only for survival and destruction. Its powers are immeasurable, its weaknesses few. Its ability to adapt to whatever kills it makes Doomsday a threat that can never truly be vanquished.

Indestructible bony protusions from its knuckles, elbows, and knees act as deadly weapons.

Doomsday's containment suit was ripped away when it emerged on Earth.

ORIGIN

Created by a scientist, Doomsday was a humanoid infant that was released onto a hellish, prehistoric Krypton. Each time the child died, its remains were used to clone a new version, with alterations to its DNA to protect it from the previous manner of its death. In time, the process became innate to the child, who also became quite insane. After slaughtering its way across the galaxy for thousands of years, the creature eventually landed on Earth, where it battled Superman and the Justice League.

"Rrraaarrr!"
DOOMSDAY

FATAL COUNTDOWN

During their first encounter with the unstoppable Doomsday, the entire Justice League—and the surrounding war zone—were decimated. During the fight, Booster Gold gave the monster its apt name. The creature's subsequent rampage through Metropolis brought Superman into the fray. At the height of a brutal battle, Superman and Doomsday simultaneously delivered apparent killer blows. Superman was placed in a healing coma, while Doomsday, though dead, was eventually reincarnated and had now adapted to the threat of the Man of Steel, ready for the next showdown.

DATA FILE

FIRST APPEARANCE: *Superman: The Man of Steel* (Vol. 1) #17 (Nov. 1992)

AFFILIATIONS: Secret Society of Super-Villains, Suicide Squad

POWERS/ABILITIES: Super-stength, super-speed, super-stamina, invulnerability, near-immortality, healing and regeneration, immunity to telepathy, reactive adaptation

THE DOMINATORS

A race of alien scientists, the Dominators grew increasingly concerned over the rising number of genetic superhuman mutations appearing on Earth. Their response was to initiate an alliance with multiple species to eliminate this potential threat to galactic stability.

GRAY MAN

A sorcerer who caught the attention of the Lords of Order, the Gray Man was tasked with collecting the dream energy of dying mortals. Believing this to be a punishment rather than a reward as intended, the Gray Man used his power to seize dream energy from the living.

MISTER NEBULA

Kirtan-Rodd was an interior decorator who angered a Lord of Order. As punishment for his arrogance, Kirtan-Rodd was banished to a realm of madness, where he spent an eternity dreaming up new designs. Once released, he decided to redecorate reality.

MANGA KHAN

A being made of gas encased within a metal suit, Manga Khan operates as an intergalactic trader. He crossed paths with the Justice League after trying to barter a captured Mister Miracle to Darkseid. Khan is frequently found in the company of a robot named L-Ron.

SCARLET SKIER

The herald of Mister Nebula, Dren Keeg (aka the Scarlet Skier) was given the task of finding worlds in need of a makeover. The Skier detests his job, and is always trying to quit. At one point, the Skier came into conflict with G'nort, the most incompetent of Green Lanterns, whom he eventually befriended after getting stranded on Earth.

STRANGER THINGS

With most of the Justice League's original members absent from the roster, Earth began once again to attract some of the cosmos' weirder villains. From simple nuisances to world-conquerors, these foes tested the strength and resolve of the new League.

THE EXTREMISTS

The new members of Justice League Europe are put to their first true test when villains from the ruined world of Angor attempt to conquer the people of Earth.

Justice League Europe (Vol. 1) #15 (Jun. 1990)
Silver Sorceress returns to the ruins of her home planet.

REFUGEES OF ANGOR

After an extended period time-traveling to other worlds in the multiverse, the Silver Sorceress—one of the surviving Champions of Angor—musters the courage to return to her shattered planet. Meanwhile, her teammate Blue Jay escapes confinement from an illegal superhuman prison. He seeks asylum at the Justice League International's Russian embassy, narrowly evading recapture by the League's bureau chief and liaison Boris Razumihin.

CONFRONTATION

The Silver Sorceress is captured by the Extremists, a group of vicious villains who destroyed Angor by initiating a nuclear holocaust. She is tortured into revealing the secret magical spell that enables her to travel between dimensions. Though he is certain he can replicate the spell, the mystically inclined Extremist Dreamslayer suggests that they keep Silver Sorceress alive in case she can be of any further use.

Justice League Europe (Vol. 1) #15 (Jun. 1990)
Tortured by Gorgon's tentacles, Silver Sorceress tries to resist.

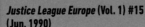

"Speak to us Uncle Mitch! Are we wacky enough for you?"

LORD HAVOK

ARMS RACE

Arriving on Earth, the Extremists rampage through Moscow. There, they are confronted by the European branch of the Justice League. The battle ends quickly, with the JLE rendered unconscious by their brutal foes. Driven to cause destruction, the team of villains makes a dangerous discovery: this Earth has its own nuclear weapons stockpile. Seeking to repeat the horrific acts that led to the annihilation of their own planet, the Extremists take control of Earth's deadly missiles, placing them in orbit. They then state their terms: humanity will serve as slaves, or perish in a nuclear holocaust.

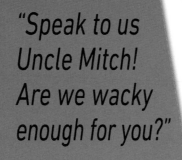

POOR PLANNING

When the governments of Earth agree to the terms of the Extremists, the JLE takes matters into its own hands. Attacking the villains, they manage to gain the upper hand. However, their advantage is short-lived. With Metamorpho encasing Dr. Diehard, negating his powers, there is nothing keeping Earth's nuclear arsenal aloft. After the villains stop the crashing missiles, they dismiss the JLE, sending them to join the Silver Sorceress on Angor—more specifically, in the amusement park Wacky World.

UNAMUSED

In the amusement park on the ruined planet, the JLE learns the truth. Other than Dreamslayer, the Extremists did not survive the nuclear holocaust they ignited. The villains the League have been fighting are in fact android duplicates built by the amusement park. Discovering the theme park's creator, Mitch Wacky, alive in suspended animation, the League devises a plan. Reviving Wacky, who can control his robot creations, they return to Earth and shut down the android beings. This leaves only Dreamslayer to be beaten by the Silver Sorceress.

JUSTICE LEAGUE TASK FORCE

Needing a dedicated, on-call strike team to serve the collective needs of world governments, the UN organized a covert squad within the ranks of the Justice League. Working from the shadows, this Task Force took on unpopular missions that the public team could not.

LEAGUE OF SHADOWS

The black ops nature of the Task Force's missions saw the team's roster undergo many changes. Over time, the group's focus shifted, with the Martian Manhunter adopting the team as a personal project, seeing his teammates as students. This role was tested when Triumph, a forgotten hero and founding member of the Justice League, returned from a dimensional limbo and quickly got on the wrong side of J'onn J'onzz. The group endured several tragedies, including the deaths of female members Ice and Mystek, and was eventually dissolved.

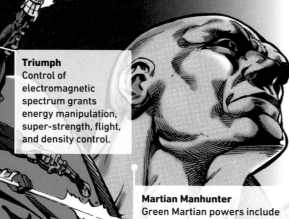

Triumph
Control of electromagnetic spectrum grants energy manipulation, super-strength, flight, and density control.

Martian Manhunter
Green Martian powers include super-strength, flight, shape-shifting, optic force beams, and telepathy.

Gypsy
Mystical illusion-casting, light bending, sound projection.

L-Ron/Despero
L-Ron's robotic mind transplanted into Despero's body grants him control of the villain's many abilities.

Ray
Ability to absorb and project light energy, create hard light constructs, and fly.

Hard target

While working with the JL Task Force, Nightwing is forced to choose between executing a terrorist to save lives or standing aside. Unable to kill, even when the target is a mass murderer, Nightwing follows his conscience—exactly as his handlers at the UN expected.

Mystek
Control over sub-atomic "quarks" grants energy manipulation, flight, and blast power.

Maxima
Alien Almeracian powers include psychokinesis, super-speed, teleportation, and telepathy.

Captain Atom
Quantum field control enables chronokinesis, energy projection, flight, and teleportation.

DRASTIC MEASURES

Led by Captain Atom, Extreme Justice battled the Legion of Doom, the time-altering villain Monarch, and the demonic entity Neron. In their determination to deliver harsh justice, the team unwittingly committed manslaughter, killing several super-villains in the nation of Bialya. This act of violence outraged the world and led to the dissolution of all operational incarnations of the Justice League.

Blue Beetle
Genius-level intellect, expert acrobat and martial artist.

Booster Gold
Power suit enables super-strength, force field generation, and time travel.

Amazing Man
Ability to duplicate any inorganic matter, absorbs and wields energy and magnetism.

Buying time

When Captain Atom is seemingly destroyed by the mysterious Mister Synge and his robots, Blue Beetle devises a counter attack. He has Amazing Man absorb just enough of Maxima's telepathic powers to enable Extreme Justice to fight on two fronts—but the team falters. As defeat seems certain, Captain Atom suddenly returns to the fray. His earlier run-in with Synge's robots had not killed him, but rather sent him minutes into the future. With Atom back in action, the tide of battle turns in favour of Extreme Justice.

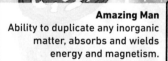

EXTREME JUSTICE

When several members of Justice League International became frustrated with UN bureaucracy, they formed a rogue team of heroes that was unafraid to cross the line and dispense Extreme Justice.

THE WATCHTOWER

Built on the Moon using a combination of Kryptonian, Martian, and Thanagarian technologies, the Watchtower served as a secure base of operations for a new incarnation of the League. As indicated by their headquarters, this team operated independently of Earth's governments.

MEMBERS

Superman

Batman

Wonder Woman

Aquaman

Green Lantern (Kyle Rayner)

Martian Manhunter

The Flash (Wally West)

Tomorrow Woman

Aztek

Green Arrow (Connor Hawke)

Plastic Man

Wonder Woman (Hippolyta)

Huntress

Steel (John Henry Irons)

Oracle

Zauriel

Big Barda

Orion

Hourman

Faith

Green Lantern (John Stewart)

Manitou Raven

Familiar names, new faces
While most of the original League reunited at this time, Kid Flash (Wally West) took the role of his predecessor, Kyle Rayner joined the League as a rookie Green Lantern, Connor Hawke came on board as Green Arrow, and John Henry Irons impressed as a very different Steel.

EYES ON THE WORLD

At the heart of the Watchtower was the Monitor Womb, which housed the League's extensive surveillance network, used to track worldwide threats on holographic displays. Batman also uses the chamber to plan and strategize. Additionally, the Watchtower boasts advanced teleportation technology no longer limited to predetermined locations, several spaceships in the base's hangar, a hydroponic garden supplying oxygen, and secure containment cells. And in a break from previous headquarters, the facility was open to public tours.

STATIONARY TARGET

Unfortunately, the widely known location of the headquarters led to frequent super-villain attacks. After the second incarnation of the Watchtower was destroyed by a parallel Earth version of Superboy, the Justice League abandoned the concept of a publicly known lunar base of operations.

A MIDSUMMER'S NIGHTMARE

Empowered by a Controller—an offshoot of the Guardians of Oa—a primitive human at the dawn of mankind was transformed into Know Man. This godlike entity is desperate to protect humanity from an oncoming cosmic threat. He claims he must play this role because the members of the Justice League have refused to fulfil their destiny and become gods.

Justice League: A Midsummer's Nightmare (Vol. 1) #2 (Oct. 1996)
Know Man's superhuman agents face down the Justice League.

POWERLESS

Justice League: A Midsummer's Nightmare (Vol. 1) #1 (Sep. 1996)
No longer The Flash, Wally West wakes from a dream of running at super-speed.

Awakening to a world where everyone has a "spark"—a genetic switch that gives them superpowers—seven heroes struggle to understand what has happened. This group—five of the original Justice League, as well as the second Flash and the newest Green Lantern—are among the only beings on Earth not to have powers. They have no recollection that the world was ever any different, but each is plagued by visions and dreams of an alternate life.

MUTANT MAYHEM

Aware that the Justice League has awoken, the enemy responsible for the sudden power surge in humanity sends a team of his own agents to battle the heroes. Several mutated humans, granted extraordinary powers via the genetic spark, ambush the team. It is a brief fight, for although the newly superpowered people are strong, they lack experience. For the League, this is a major concern; humanity as a whole cannot safely be entrusted with such power.

DESTINY REVEALED

Seeking each other out, the heroes slowly recall the existence that was once theirs. As they do, their own powers return. Using the Martian Manhunter's telepathic abilities to probe the mind of Green Lantern, the group discovers that an old villain is sending them all messages. Doctor Destiny, imprisoned in a remote, fortified location, is trying to reach the seven heroes with whom he is most familiar—the original lineup of the League.

Justice League: A Midsummer's Nightmare (Vol. 1) #3 (Nov. 1996)
J'onn J'onzz unlocks Kyle Rayner's mind.

Justice League: A Midsummer's Nightmare **(Vol. 1) #3 (Nov. 1996)**
The hidden power behind events reveals himself—Know Man.

"It will come suddenly, and without warning."

KNOW MAN

Justice League: A Midsummer's Nightmare **(Vol. 1) #3 (Nov. 1996)**
The League regain their senses with the Lasso of Truth.

BEST INTENTIONS

After fighting their way through to the military complex where Destiny is held, the group rescues the imprisoned villain. It is then that they come face to face with their true opponent—a being called Know Man. He claims that he must empower all of humanity as a means of protecting Earth from a cosmic threat called Mageddon. The League dismisses these concerns and battles the powerful immortal, who attacks each hero in the depths of their own minds.

FUTURE FEARS

Saved through the Martian Manhunter's compassion and the magic of Wonder Woman's lasso, the team escape their mental prisons. Seeing his plans unravel, Know Man stands down, reversing all he has done to humanity in the process. With his final words, he warns the heroes that the fate of the future is now in their hands, and states that he hopes they will be up to the task. In light of these events, the original League reforms, and prepares to once again become protectors of Earth.

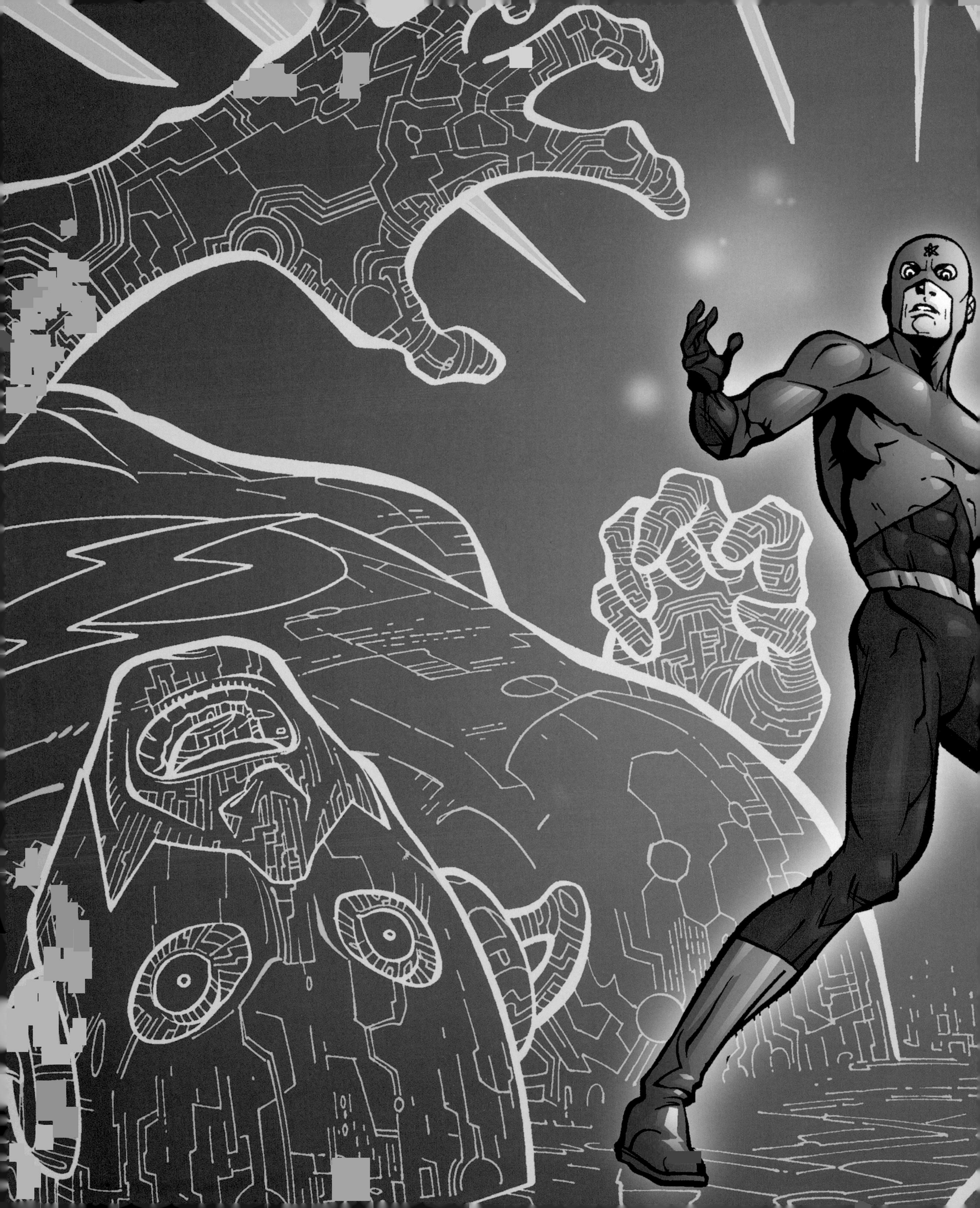

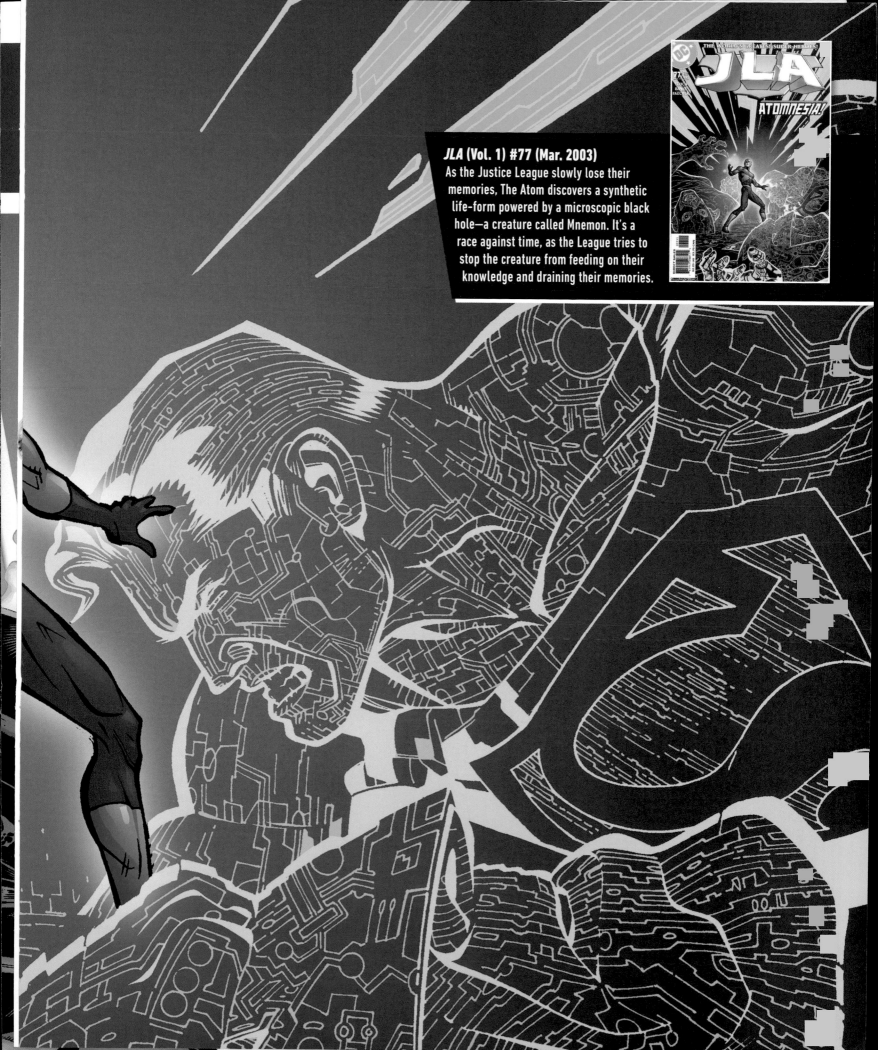

JLA (Vol. 1) #77 (Mar. 2003)
As the Justice League slowly lose their memories, The Atom discovers a synthetic life-form powered by a microscopic black hole—a creature called Mnemon. It's a race against time, as the League tries to stop the creature from feeding on their knowledge and draining their memories.

THE HYPERCLAN

They arrived in a blaze of publicity, announcing themselves as the saviors of mankind. To that end, the Hyperclan set about greening deserts and, to the alarm of the Justice League, executing super-villians. However, these alien rivals to the League had a more sinister purpose: in reality they were White Martians out to conquer Earth.

> "We are the **Hyperclan**. We have come to save the world."
>
> PROTEX

INVADERS FROM MARS

The first wave of a White Martian invasion force, posing as a benevolent Super Hero team, the Hyperclan used their Martian powers to assume human-like forms. They projected feelings of trust and obedience onto the unsuspecting population of Earth. Uncovered by the newly formed incarnation of the Justice League, the Hyperclan, and the thousands of White Martians they led, were defeated and brainwashed into forgetting their alien nature.

PRIMAID

Primaid describes herself as "a true Martian soldier," one with absolute contempt for the Green Martians. She can use her shape-changing skills to learn multiple battle configurations, and can focus her considerable strength enough to injure Superman.

ZÜM

Channeling the bulk of his Martian powers into his speed, Züm is able to reach a velocity close to that of the third incarnation of The Flash, Wally West. In addition, he has had military training in the use of his powers, and is willing to kill.

A-MORTAL

Less confident in the certainty of their victory than his comrades, A-Mortal's behavior borders on the paranoid. Although he has adopted a ghoulish form, he tends to use his powers in the most basic manner—super-strength, flight, and speed.

PROTEX

The leader of the Hyperclan, Protex is a Martian telepath who is powerful enough to manipulate the emotions of the entire population of Earth. So great is his skill that he was even able to weaken and capture Superman with imaginary Kryptonite. However, the Man of Steel saw through the ruse and escaped.

ZENTURION

Arming himself with a shield and an energy whip, Zenturion carries himself like a warrior. He relies on his exceptional skill in weaponized combat first, and his natural-born Martian powers second. Both Green Lantern and The Flash found him to be a very tough customer.

ARMEK

Assuming the form of a massive mech-warrior, Armek invests himself heavily in the physical nature of his role. He was bitterly angry when the Martian Manhunter copied the shape he had designed.

TRONIX

One of the most bloodthirsty members of the Hyperclan, Tronix has openly bragged about the murders she has committed, and takes pride in the injuries she has inflicted. Like most sadistic beings, she prefers an unfair fight in her favor.

FLUXUS

Choosing to rely on his shape-changing skill in combat, Fluxus is expert at realistically adapting his form to those of his opponents. It is a power he uses to strike when his foes least expect it—a method he prefers to direct conflict.

IDENTITY CRISIS

The secret identity of a hero is their most precious possession. Not just because of the need to escape the furiously paced life of crime-fighting, but to protect loved ones from retribution at the hands of criminals. But no matter how tightly the members of the Justice League cling to their secrets, they cannot keep everyone safe...

Identity Crisis (Vol. 1) #2 (Sep. 2004)
The villainous Deathstroke the Terminator stands defiantly between the Justice League and his employer, Doctor Light.

SENSELESS VIOLENCE

On a stakeout, Elongated Man receives a distressing emergency call from his wife, Sue Dibny. She is being savagely attacked by a mysterious figure, one she is unable to identify. Though he rushes home as quickly as he can, Elongated Man is too late to save his wife. He arrives at his house to find Sue dead, horribly burned by her assailant.

Identity Crisis (Vol. 1) #1 (Aug. 2004)
Brutally assaulted by an unknown assailant, Sue Dibny has moments to live.

A DEEPER MYSTERY

The world's heroes investigate, but can find no trace of the killer's identity at the scene of the crime. Several League members have reason to suspect that Doctor Light, a villain who assaulted Sue many years before, might have struck at her in revenge. Light, knowing he is under suspicion, hires the mercenary Deathstroke as his guardian. It takes the combined might of the League to bring down Deathstroke and capture Light—who is then proven innocent!

Identity Crisis (Vol. 1) #1 (Aug. 2004)
The world's heroes assemble in church to lay Sue Dibny to rest.

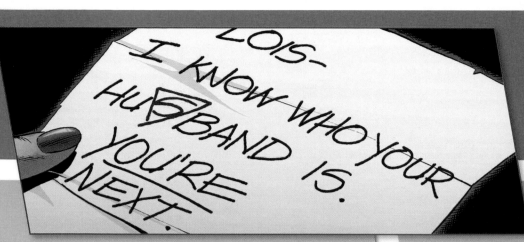

Identity Crisis (Vol. 1) #4
(Nov. 2004)
*An anonymous note
sends a shockwave of
fear through Lois Lane.*

SERIAL KILLER

Another violent assault occurs. Jean Loring, the ex-wife of The Atom, is attacked in her home and nearly strangled. Although The Atom arrives in time, many of the heroes are rattled, believing that the mysterious killer might target any of their loved ones next. It's a fear that is well justified, as Lois Lane soon receives a threatening message.

> "This is the part where
> you're supposed to kiss me."
>
> JEAN LORING

THE PLOT THICKENS

While no attack on Lois occurs, there is another death. Jack Drake, father of the current Robin, receives a warning package with a pistol at his home. He is then killed in a stand-off during an unlikely assault by a third-rate villain called Captain Boomerang, who bungles his assassination attempt and is shot by Drake. Many heroes assume that the case is closed, but Dr. Mid-Nite discovers horrific clues during Sue's autopsy—microscopic footprints!

AN UNFORGIVEABLE ACT

In the end, the real murderer is revealed as the one who stood to profit the most. Jean Loring, desperate to recapture her husband's heart, assumed that a murder of a hero's loved one would drive couples closer together—an insane theory that proved correct. Faking her own attack brought her more attention, and then the attack on Jack Drake and the death of the supposed "killer" wrapped the case up. But her use of a spare Atom suit gives away her identity, and soon she is placed in an asylum.

Identity Crisis
(Vol. 1) #7
(Feb. 2005)
*As her insane
scheme to
win back
The Atom
unravels,
Jean Loring
is driven to
madness.*

For his part, a distraught and despairing Elongated Man attempts to see his wife Sue resurrected, but instead follows her to an untimely death.

Identity Crisis (Vol. 1) #5 (Dec. 2004)
After a brief struggle, Jack Drake and Captain Boomerang lie dead.

KEY CHARACTERS

JUSTICE LEAGUE ELITE

Once again, the League faced the need to operate just outside the law, delivering the kind of brutal punishment the general public might look upon with alarm. Though the team had walked this fine line between law and justice before, this time they discovered that doing what is right is not necessarily the same as doing the right thing.

ELITE FORCE

Justice League Elite began life as a covert, violent assembly of antiheroes led by the ruthless telepath Manchester Black. Following Black's death, his sister Vera reorganized the group as a clandestine arm of the JLA that crossed lines that the public branch could not. However, things deteriorated quickly as the group's extreme personalities fractured the team, leading to Manitou Raven's death. It was finally revealed that the malign spirit of her brother may have poisoned Vera's mind. After ridding herself of his dark influence, she ended the "grand experiment," and Justice League Elite was no more.

Major Disaster
Super-strength and can also warp cause and effect to such an extent that he can make a comet fall from orbit.

Menagerie
Controls tiny alien parasites on her body called symbeasts, transforming them into unique weapons.

Coldcast
Ability to manipulate, absorb, and generate all forms of energy.

Kasumi
Reformed assassin and near-unrivaled wielder of twin katanas, Kasumi was secretly Cassandra (Batgirl) Cain working undercover for Batman.

Naif al-Sheikh
His genius-level intellect and scrupulous integrity make Naif al-Sheikh perfect for the Elite's behind-the-scenes government liaison.

Manitou Raven
Time-displaced shaman from the Obsidian Age of Atlantis, bestowed with formidable mystical powers.

Vera Black (alias "Sister Superior")
Her powerful cyborg body stores an array of weaponry as well as holographic disguises.

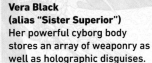

The Flash
Wally West worked with both the Justice League and the Justice League Elite, occasionally wearing a dark costume when fighting with the latter.

Green Arrow
Oliver Queen brought his legendary archery, tactical skills, and outspoken liberal views to the team.

FINAL SACRIFICE

After learning that his wife, Dawn, was having an affair with Green Arrow, Manitou Raven focused on the team's mission—to stop the villain Aftermath from obtaining the map of the universe. But when his teammate Major Disaster was unable to prevent an explosion while in pursuit of their quarry, Raven seized the moment, sacrificing his life to shield his teammates from the blast.

148

JUSTICE LEAGUES

After alien invaders alter the memories of everyone on Earth, the Justice League was forgotten—even by the League itself. However, each League member remained vaguely aware of the team that they were once part of, and began creating their own version of the Justice League.

JUSTICE LEAGUE OF ATLANTIS

To protect his underwater kingdom from the threats of air-breathers, Aquaman recruited Tempest, Mera, Arion, Lori Lemaris, Devilfish, and Power Girl into his Justice League of Atlantis.

JUSTICE LEAGUE OF ARKHAM

Determined to save Gotham City, Batman formed his own unlikely, highly volatile League. He enlisted several Arkham Asylum inmates, such as Catwoman, the Riddler, Poison Ivy, the Ventriloquist, and the Joker.

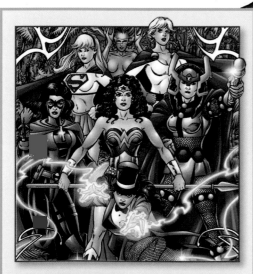

JUSTICE LEAGUE OF AMAZONS

The goal of the Justice League of Amazons was to protect and defend Mother Earth and her children. Led by Wonder Woman, members included Supergirl, Huntress, Big Barda, Zatanna, and Black Orchid.

JUSTICE LEAGUE OF ALIENS

To prove that not all extraterrestrials were evil, the Martian Manhunter assembled the Justice League of Aliens. The team included Superman, Orion, Starfire, Lobo, Guy Gardner, and Starman.

OTHER LEAGUES

Elsewhere, other Leagues were established. Kyle Rayner established the Justice League of Air for flying heroes; Zauriel gathered together spiritual beings for the Justice League of Apostles; The Flash headed up the Justice League of Adventure, and Plastic Man brought together the chaotic Justice League of Anarchy.

C risis after crisis, war after war, the Justice League battled on, one cataclysmic event colliding into another with barely any respite. It was a testing time for the world, as its heroes were forced to settle for holding back the growing tide of darkness rather than defeating it.

THE HEROES FALL

JLA (Vol. 2) #43 (May 2010)
The older members of the Justice League retire,
as many of the team's former sidekicks join.

JLA (Vol. 2) #49 (Nov. 2010)
A villain known as the Bogeyman forces members
of the League to fight their childhood friends.

JLA (Vol. 2) #52 (Feb. 2011)
In a battle against the Crime
Syndicate, Supergirl is tempted
by her darker self.

JLA (Vol. 2) #60 (Oct. 2011)
Dick Grayson, as Batman and Justice League leader,
shuts down the team, ending an era.

HALL OF JUSTICE

Designed by Wonder Woman and John Stewart, the Hall of Justice used reality-warping technology to move sideways through space, allowing for a base on Earth and an orbital satellite. Now the League could be accessible to the public, and have a secure location from which to defend the planet.

MEMBERS

Superman

Batman

Wonder Woman

Black Canary

Green Lantern (Hal Jordan)

Hawkgirl

Red Tornado

Black Lightning

Red Arrow

Vixen

Green Lantern (John Stewart)

Firestorm

The Atom

Green Arrow

Supergirl

Congorilla

Starman

Doctor Light

Mon-El

Donna Troy

Guardian

Batman (Dick Grayson)

Starfire

Cyborg

Plastic Man

Jade

Jesse Quick

Passing the torch
Membership during the time the League was based in the Hall of Justice fluctuated frequently. The final incarnation was led by the new Batman, Dick Grayson, whose team was largely made up of former sidekicks who had assumed the roles of their mentors.

TRIUMPHS AND TROPHIES

Knowing that the Justice League needed to work with mankind as much as it needed to operate as a line of defense, the team built its new headquarters on Earth with visitors in mind. The structure featured a large trophy room filled with replicas from the League's many adventures. In contrast, all available space on the satellite was dedicated to function— with a high-tech training facility nicknamed "The Kitchen."

ORBITAL JUSTICE

The new satellite half of the League's headquarters was heavily armed with both offensive and defensive weaponry. These were designed to withstand galactic-level threats, a theory sorely tested when an army of Yellow Lanterns led by Sinestro attacked and were only just repelled. The base survived many onslaughts, but was finally powered down when the Justice League disbanded.

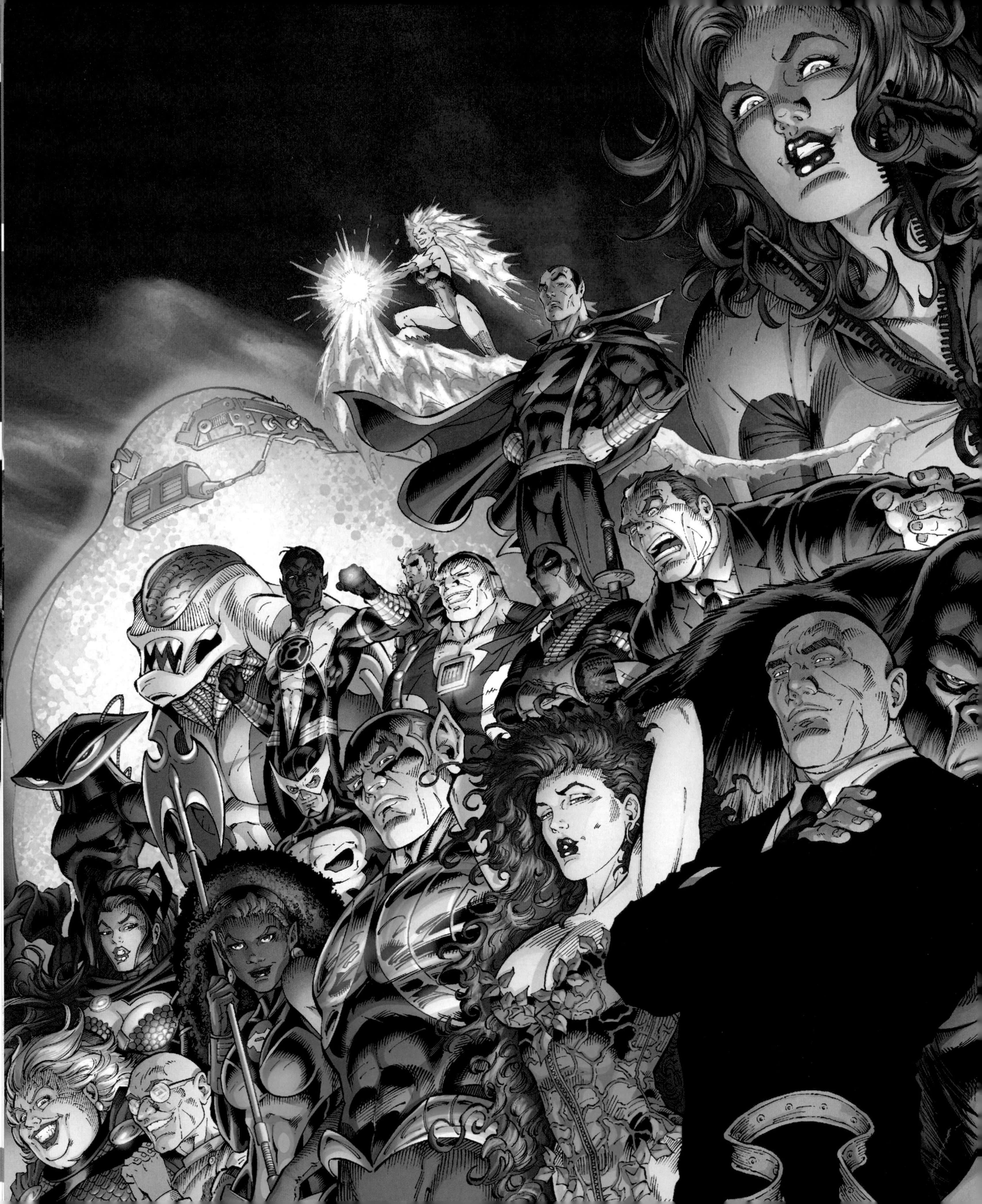

Justice League of America (Vol. 2) #13 (Nov. 2007)
A new incarnation of the Injustice League rises, as the most dangerous and notorious villains in the universe form an unholy alliance. Their common goal: to destroy their heroic counterparts, by all means necessary and no matter what the cost.

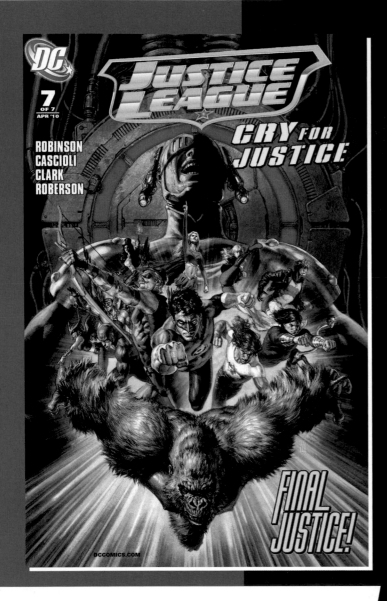

APRIL 2010

MAIN CHARACTERS

Green Lantern • Green Arrow • Supergirl • Red Arrow • Shazam • Miss Martian • Congorilla • Shade • Starman • The Flash • The Atom • Donna Troy • Starfire • Animal Man • Black Canary • Speedy • Vixen

MAIN LOCATIONS

Hall of Justice • Star City • Fawcett City • Opal City • Central City • Keystone City • Limbo

JUSTICE LEAGUE: CRY FOR JUSTICE #7

PROMETHEUS OUTWITS THE JUSTICE LEAGUE—BUT PAYS A TERRIBLE PRICE.

Concerned by the apparent deaths of Batman and the Martian Manhunter, Green Lantern and Green Arrow leave the League to take a more proactive approach toward fighting crime. Teaming up with other heroes, the pair are manipulated by the villain Prometheus, who maims Green Arrow's sidekick, Red Arrow.

1 Though the League has captured Prometheus, the villain has a contingency plan. He has spread bombs across the globe, including one that has already detonated in Green Arrow's hometown, Star City! The heroes rush to stop the devastation, but arrive too late to save Red Arrow's young daughter, Lian.

2 Prometheus demands a trade. If he is granted his freedom, he will halt the destruction. With thousands already dead, and more lives certain to be lost, the League tries every method they can think of to extract the information they need from Prometheus in order to save the world.

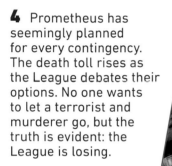

"God help me I'll kill you!"

GREEN ARROW

3 Miss Martian attempts to access Prometheus' mind, to no avail. Shazam tries his magic lightning, but instead of ending the destruction, accelerates it. Every move the League makes meets with failure.

4 Prometheus has seemingly planned for every contingency. The death toll rises as the League debates their options. No one wants to let a terrorist and murderer go, but the truth is evident: the League is losing.

5 The decision is finally made by Green Arrow. Though he has already seen his sidekick maimed and his granddaughter-in-spirit die, he argues that there is no way the League can reasonably let more innocents perish. The order is given, and Prometheus is released—just as the villain planned.

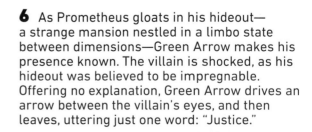

6 As Prometheus gloats in his hideout— a strange mansion nestled in a limbo state between dimensions—Green Arrow makes his presence known. The villain is shocked, as his hideout was believed to be impregnable. Offering no explanation, Green Arrow drives an arrow between the villain's eyes, and then leaves, uttering just one word: "Justice."

FLASHPOINT

When the recently resurrected Barry Allen's past is manipulated by a villain, the hero pushes his powers to breaking point to outrace tragedy—with dire consequences for the entire universe.

UNLOCKING EVIL

Running backward through time, Zoom, aka the Reverse-Flash, visits The Flash's childhood and murders his mother. Unable to cope with a loss that now haunts him, Barry follows Zoom back in time and stops him. The change to Barry's personal timeline causes a ripple effect that alters everything the hero has ever known, starting with the history of his teammates in the Justice League.

Flashpoint (Vol. 2) #1 (Jul. 2011)
Barry Allen speeds through time to prevent his mother's death.

Flashpoint (Vol. 2) #4 (Oct. 2011)
Enraged at the murder of his wife, Mera, Aquaman attacks her killer, Wonder Woman, as all around Amazons battle Atlanteans.

TEAM BATTLE

After the assassination of Queen Hippolyta at a royal wedding between Wonder Woman of Themyscira and Aquaman of Atlantis, the two previously hidden nations go to war. It is a terrible conflict that quickly tears apart the world, leading to mass death and destruction. Radically changed in this rewritten universe, Wonder Woman murders both Mera of Atlantis and Steve Trevor—a man that in her previous existence she had loved.

Flashpoint (Vol. 2) #2 (Aug. 2011)
Standing with the Batman of this altered Earth, Barry Allen is overwhelmed by memories of the new timeline.

Flashpoint (Vol. 2) #1 (Jul. 2011)
Batman—Thomas Wayne—makes short work of Batcave interloper Barry Allen.

> "What are you doing?! Let me go! I have to save her!"
>
> THE FLASH

UNEXPECTED VICTORY

Powerless in this corrupted timeline, The Flash finds an ally in Batman. A different hero than the one The Flash remembers, this Batman is Bruce Wayne's father, Thomas, who witnessed his wife and child die at the hands of a gunman. Convinced by The Flash that there is a chance that his son could live, Thomas Wayne agrees to help Barry regain his speed so that he can undo what he has wrought.

CALCULATED EFFORT

To save the world, Barry must run back into his own past and stop himself from saving his mother—thus restoring the already damaged timeline created by the Reverse-Flash. Though it breaks his heart, the speedster does what he must. However, as history begins to revert to its natural order, another force is exerted on time, one that causes many familiar aspects of the world to shift again. Time is written and rewritten, and a new reality is born. The history of the Justice League and the heroes of the world is undone, only to restart once again from the beginning.

Flashpoint (Vol. 2) #5 (Oct. 2011)
To keep the nightmarish alternate Earth from coming to pass, The Flash races to stop himself changing history.

Flashpoint (Vol. 2) #3 (Sep. 2011)
On this altered Earth, Clark Kent grew up in captivity at the Project: Superman facility deep beneath New Metropolis.

REVENGE OF THE PAST

Teaming up with Cyborg, The Flash and Batman seek out another ally—Superman. Although only The Flash recalls the Man of Steel, Barry is convinced that the effort to reverse the effects on the timestream will be aided by the Kryptonian hero. However, what they find in this reality is very different to the Superman of the past. Here, Clark Kent was kept in confinement his entire life, away from the solar energy that would empower him. Meanwhile, the war between Atlantis and the Amazons escalates, taking the lives of many heroes.

The world had been reshaped, rebuilt through the machinations of cosmic entities far beyond the power of mere mortals. Within this new reality, the Justice League was reborn anew, familiar faces in long-established roles, yet meeting for the very first time.

A WORLD REBORN

Justice League (Vol. 2) #12 (Oct. 2012)
Superman and Wonder Woman discover that their
feelings for each other have become stronger.

Justice League (Vol. 2) #20 (Dec. 2014)
The Amazo virus spreads, and no one, not even the
Justice League, is safe from its effects.

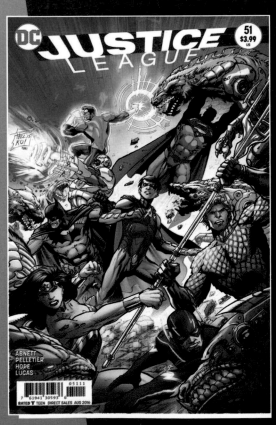

JL (Vol. 2) #51 (Aug. 2016)
Dick Grayson, the original Robin,
proves his mettle to the League
for the first time.

Justice League (Vol. 3) #3 (Oct. 2016)
The reborn League struggles against the Awakened,
a powerful, ancient evil determined to destroy
them and reclaim the universe.

THE NEW WATCHTOWER

Reborn into a new reality, the Justice League once again stationed themselves within a satellite headquarters called the Watchtower. Although the origins of this orbital base remain unknown, its purpose—to serve as a defensive line for the Earth from the perils of space, while also monitoring the planet below for homegrown threats—is a familiar one.

MEMBERS

Superman

Batman

Wonder Woman

Green Lantern
(Hal Jordan)

Cyborg

Aquaman

The Flash
(Barry Allen)

Element Woman

The Atom
(Rhonda Pineda)

Firestorm

Shazam

Lex Luthor

Captain Cold

Green Lantern
(Jessica Cruz)

Green Lantern
(Simon Baz)

Steve Trevor
(Government Liaison)

A familiar foundation
Unifying as a team in this new universe, the Justice League's initial line-up was a recognizable one. After working together for years, the core group has only recently begun to expand its roster.

TELEPORTING INTO DANGER

With a teleportation system built from the New Gods' Boom Tube technology, the Watchtower satellite is capable of transporting members anywhere on Earth—and places beyond. Practical in design, the satellite offers little in the way of distractions or creature comforts—save for a ping-pong table Shazam inadvertently wished into existence shortly after joining the team.

FALLING TO EARTH

Post-Flashpoint, the Watchtower was destroyed by the villain Despero, who unleashed his fury on the new recruits aboard at the time. A second Watchtower was built by Lex Luthor and gifted to the League in an effort to join the team. It served them well, but after a mysterious cosmic being reshaped the multiverse, a new Watchtower took its place. However, this incarnation barely saw the light of day before it was devastated by an encryption-busting A.I. game called Genie. As the space station plummeted to earth, it was only Cyborg's quick thinking that saved San Francisco from disaster.

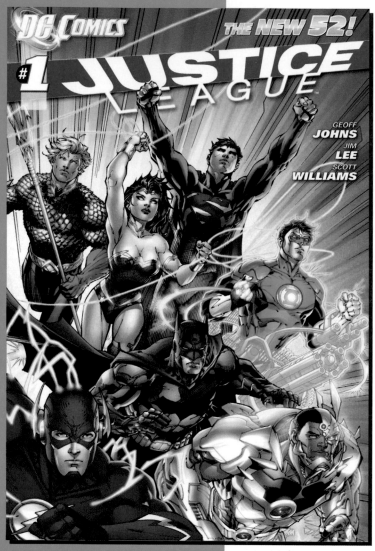

JUSTICE LEAGUE (VOL.2) #1

THE HEROES OF THE NEW UNIVERSE UNITE TO REPEL AN APOKOLIPTIAN RAID.

After the events of Flashpoint, reality has been rewritten. While the precise cause of the cosmic event remains unknown, the effects are far-reaching. In this new reality, the Justice League never came together as a team as they had before. Now, a new origin starts...

NOVEMBER 2011

MAIN CHARACTERS
Batman • Green Lantern • Superman

SUPPORTING CHARACTERS
Victor Stone

MAIN LOCATIONS
Gotham City • Metropolis

1 While tracking a strange alien creature through Gotham, Batman is interrupted by the appearance of Green Lantern. The methods of the two heroes stand in stark contrast. Green Lantern inadvertently draws the attention of the Gotham City police, who open fire on the pair.

"You're not just some guy in a bat costume, are you?"

GREEN LANTERN

3 Green Lantern learns, to his shock, that Batman has no powers. Batman in turns steals Green Lantern's ring, mocking the hero with how simple it was to disarm him. The Dark Knight deduces that the ring requires concentration to work.

2 Using his power ring to defend against the police helicopters, Green Lantern believes he has the situation under control. Unfortunately, Batman and Green Lantern are then ambushed by the hostile creature Batman had been hunting.

4 The two Super Heroes are led into the sewers in pursuit of the being from another world. The alien sacrifices itself in an explosion, uttering just two words: "For Darkseid." Deciding that one extraterrestrial might be able to help them with another, the pair seek the advice of another hero from off-world—Superman.

5 A young Victor Stone witnesses Green Lantern and Batman fly overhead during his high school football game, unaware that he will soon play a part in the formation of the Justice League as the hero Cyborg. Landing in Metropolis, Batman and Green Lantern search for the Kryptonian hero.

6 Overconfident, Green Lantern cages Batman in a prison construct and approaches Superman on his own. The meeting escalates quickly to a fight, as Superman is unfamiliar with both Batman and Green Lantern, and believes them to be enemies.

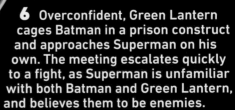

BAD GUYS AND NEW BLOOD

There were few certainties in the brave new world the Justice League now inhabited. Where once the line between hero and villain was clearly defined, now it became blurred, as criminals joined the team alongside faces old and new.

> "*The Justice League is dead. Superman is gone. This is a job for Lex Luthor.*"
>
> LEX LUTHOR

LEX LUTHOR

In a strange twist, Superman's archnemesis and longtime enemy of the Justice League briefly joined the team, manipulating his way onto the roster. As a member of the League, Lex Luthor brought an unprecedented level of scientific knowledge and a sheer tenacity to win that was almost unmatched. However, given his corrupt nature, the team knew that Luthor could not be trusted. This ongoing tension frequently undercut any real value Luthor might have brought to the team—particularly when the threats the heroes faced originated with Luthor himself.

SHAZAM

One of the heroes most affected by the reality shift after Flashpoint was Billy Batson. Now known simply as Shazam, this version of Billy lost the magical connection to the gods that gave him his powers and turned to a new group of deities, including S'ivaa, a slumbering monster god, H'ronmeer, the Martian god of death, and Zonuz, wielder of the Old Gods' Torment Sanction. Billy's switch to these new gods was only temporary.

CAPTAIN COLD

Raised in desperate poverty and badly abused, Leonard Snart grew up to become a petty criminal. After managing to get his hands on a cold gun, he soon turned his cutthroat nature and scheming mind to the role of super-villain. Despite a long history of criminal endeavors—and many battles with The Flash as one of the notorious band of villains, the Rogues—Captain Cold played a significant role defeating the Crime Syndicate and was pardoned for his crimes. He subsequently fell into the employ of Lex Luthor, who levered the villain into the role of hero alongside him to join the ranks of the Justice League.

GREEN LANTERN (JESSICA CRUZ)

After stumbling on a murder, Jessica and her friends were assaulted by mobsters. Only Jessica survived, and afterward carried deep emotional scars. When the Crime Syndicate attacked the Justice League, the evil Ring of Volthoom sought out the young woman as a potential new host. However, unlike every other servant of the ring, Jessica was able to resist its psychic influence, and took command of the sentient weapon. After the nefarious ring was destroyed, Jessica was chosen by the Green Lantern Corps to wear one of their rings. Her ordeals have taught her to finally confront and conquer the fears she had clung to for so long.

ELEMENT WOMAN

Using his database of known metahumans to enlist heroes against a threat emerging from the depths of Atlantis, Cyborg recruited Emily Sung, alias Element Woman, into the ranks of the Justice League. Her membership was quickly agreed by the rest of the team due to her unique physiology. Virtually nothing is known of her past, but she showed herself to be both loyal and reasonable, doing her best to keep the peace when tempers flared. She was badly traumatized during a battle with the Crime Syndicate, and left the League to join the Doom Patrol.

GREEN LANTERN (SIMON BAZ)

Simon Baz was a young car thief who inadvertently stole a car carrying a bomb. Upon discovering this, Baz drove the car to a remote factory so that no one would be hurt by the explosion, but was captured by the authorities and treated as a terrorist. Chosen by a malfunctioning Green Lantern ring, Baz realized he needed to step up to the challenge life had thrown at him and do his best to use the ring to help defend Earth. Eventually, his heroism landed him a role in the ranks of the Justice League, and he was appointed to be the official Green Lantern of Earth.

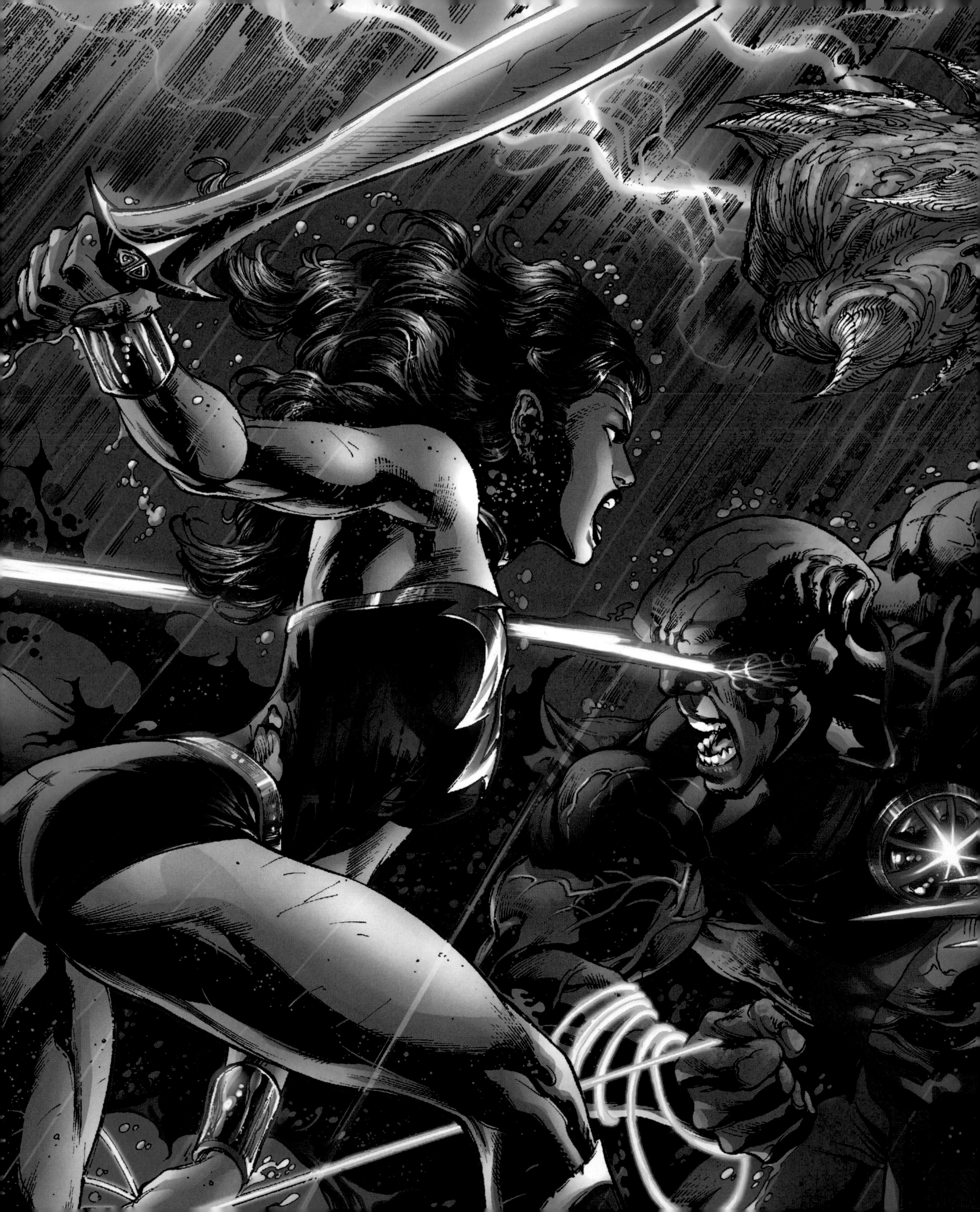

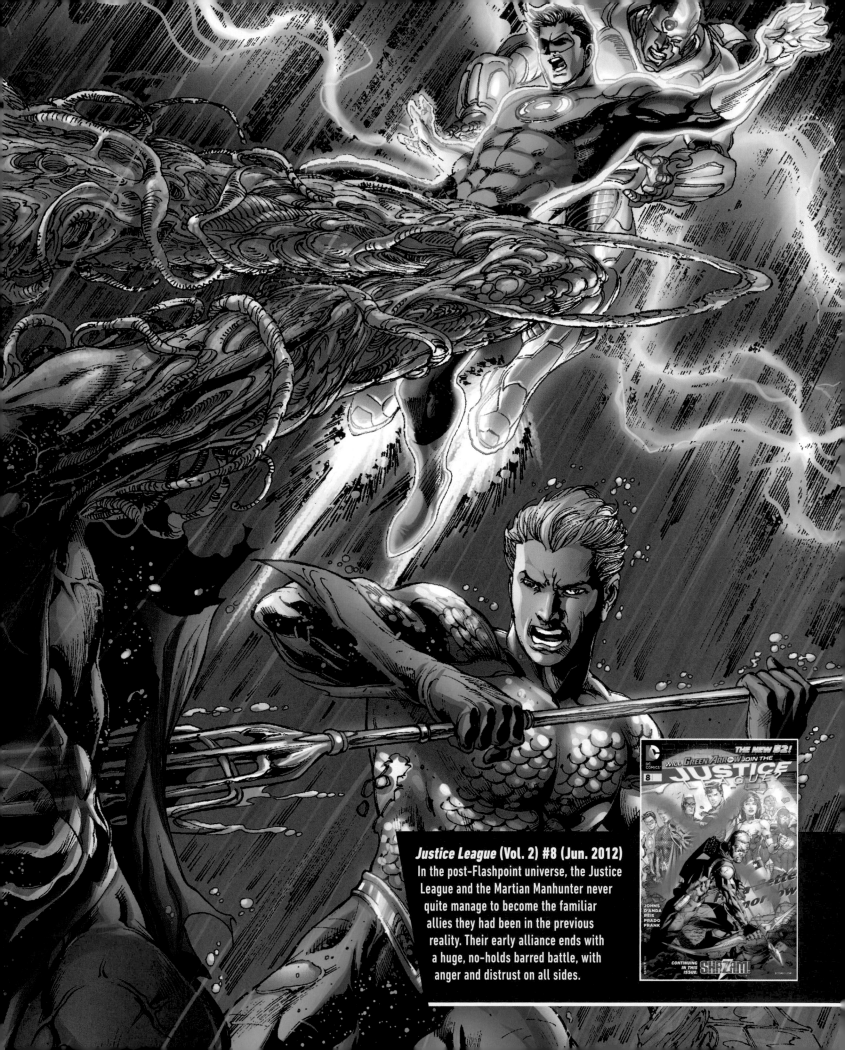

Justice League (Vol. 2) #8 (Jun. 2012)
In the post-Flashpoint universe, the Justice League and the Martian Manhunter never quite manage to become the familiar allies they had been in the previous reality. Their early alliance ends with a huge, no-holds barred battle, with anger and distrust on all sides.

MANY LEAGUES OF JUSTICE

The formation of the Justice League was a world-changing event. Across the globe, many were either inspired by this new team of heroes, or grew suspicious of their power and independence. Since then, a number of other "Leagues" have sprung up—and not always with the best intentions...

JUSTICE LEAGUES OF AMERICA

...the American Way
Led by Steve Trevor, Waller's JLA included Green Arrow, Hawkman, Green Lantern (Simon Baz), Vibe, Katana, Stargirl, the Martian Manhunter, and Catwoman.

JLA: PATRIOTIC PROTECTORS

After the reality-altering Flashpoint event, government agent Amanda Waller decided the US needed heroes who answered to the nation. She enlisted Steve Trevor, former Justice League liaison, to the new Justice League of America. It was soon clear that the JLA had been set up to counter the Justice League, in case the latter's actions ever threatened US interests. The JLA ultimately dissolved, with the more earnestly heroic members coming together as Justice League United.

JLA: DARK KNIGHT DEFENDERS

More recently, a new Justice League of America has emerged. Though still dedicated to combating domestic rather than global threats, this team was not formed out of misplaced patriotic fear. An offshoot of the official Justice League, the group is led by Batman. The idea for the team occurred to the Dark Knight after he grudgingly saw the wisdom of Amanda Waller's Task Force X, alias the Suicide Squad. This incarnation of the JLA includes Killer Frost, Lobo, Black Canary, Vixen, The Atom, and the Ray.

JUSTICE LEAGUE UNITED

After accepting the fact that the Justice League of America they had been a part of was created for less than noble purposes, Stargirl and several other heroes formed the Justice League United. The team, whose members included Adam and Alanna Strange, Animal Man, and Equinox, only operated for a short time, the majority of its adventures occurring either in Canada or on distant worlds in the depths of space.

JUSTICE LEAGUE DARK

Assembling the world's foremost mystic practitioners, the Justice League Dark first gathered when magical events began wreaking havoc across the globe. These incidents were triggered when the Enchantress' mystical persona separated from her human host, June Moone. Brought together by Madame Xanadu, the team included Swamp Thing, John Constantine, Zatanna, Deadman, Frankenstein, and Shade the Changing Man. As they established themselves, the group took up residence in the House of Mystery, a living building containing unimaginable horrors.

JUSTICE LEAGUE 3000

In the 31st Century, the Cadmus corporation, a company famed for its experiments in genetic engineering, designed a way to utilize the Justice League's stored DNA. This was turned into a form of infection that could be injected into a host body, rewriting its genetic structure. In this way, the original Justice League was resurrected, after a fashion. While the cloned team possessed some of the original members' memories and powers, they lacked the emotional experience that bound the original League together. The group's cohesion—and effectiveness—was further impaired by Cadmus making new genetic copies of team members who were killed in action.

DARKSEID WAR

"I'm a god now."
BATMAN

The ultimate battle between the Justice League's two most dangerous cosmic foes has begun. The immensely powerful antimatter being known as the Anti-Monitor has initiated a war upon Darkseid, the Dark Lord of Apokolips. Life, death, and the power of the gods is at stake.

Justice League (Vol. 2) #42 (Sep. 2015)
Batman assumes control of the Mobius Chair and, through it, all information in the universe.

KNOWLEDGE IS POWER

Metron, the God of Knowledge, transports the League to a safe haven. Sensing an opportunity, Batman takes control of the Mobius Chair—a mysterious device Metron uses to travel across time and space—seizing the power of ultimate knowledge for himself. Meanwhile, Superman is lost on Apokolips, where he is forced into one of the planet's fabled fire pits. The raging inferno supercharges the Kryptonian's cell structure, making him powerful beyond measure.

Justice League (Vol. 2) #44 (Nov. 2015)
As Darkseid and the Anti-Monitor wage a war that has been an eternity in the making, the Justice League does what it can to keep the Earth safe.

Justice League (Vol. 2) #42 (Sep. 2015)
Wonder Woman prepares to battle Grail; a battle that is abruptly interrupted by the appearance of the Anti-Monitor.

OMINOUS ARRIVAL

While investigating indications of Apokoliptian technology being used on Earth, the Justice League is ambushed by a woman who calls herself Grail and claims to be the daughter of Darkseid. Grail uses the Earth-3 Ring of Volthoom worn by Justice Leaguer Jessica Cruz to open the way for an even greater threat—the arrival of the Anti-Monitor.

Justice League (Vol. 2) #44 (Nov. 2015)
Using the Anti-Life Equation, the Anti-Monitor achieves the impossible—he strikes down Darkseid, whose death is assured by the presence of the Black Racer.

Justice League (Vol. 2) #47 Feb. 2016
Freed from the Anti-Life Equation, the Anti-Monitor becomes Mobius once more—a transformation that makes him even more dangerous.

A RACE WITH DEATH

Grail lures Darkseid and his minions to Earth, and soon the cataclysmic battle against the Anti-Monitor and his Qwardian army is joined. As the cosmic war rages, the Justice League tries to minimize casualties by slowing down both titanic enemies. Frustrated, Darkseid summons the spirit of Death—the Black Racer. But this proves to be Darkseid's undoing, as the Anti-Monitor seizes control of Death and fuses it with The Flash, forcing the speedster to destroy the lord of Apokolips.

REVERSION OF FORM

A rebel group on Apokolips captures Darkseid's devastating Omega Effect and imprisons it within Lex Luthor, turning him into the heir of Apokolips. Elsewhere, the Anti-Monitor enters a cocoon stage, separating from the Anti-Life Equation and reverting to his original form—the being known as Mobius. Amid this chaos, Jessica Cruz is overwhelmed by the Ring of Volthoom and releases the Crime Syndicate from prison, including the pregnant Superwoman.

DARK SEED

The newly freed Crime Syndicate joins the fight and Superwoman's child is born on the battlefield. However, Grail betrays and kills Mobius, using the newborn's natural powers to absorb the Anti-Life Equation, as well as the powers of the New Gods the Justice League had absorbed. The infant is Darkseid born anew, and Grail disappears with him, vowing to raise her father with love, and give him a second chance at life.

Justice League (Vol. 2) #50 (May 2016)
Even as a reborn infant, Darkseid hungers for power. Only time will tell if his daughter can alter his true nature.

EVIL REAWAKENS

The new Earth created in the wake of the Flashpoint event had transformed the history of the League's villains. Many of them were reborn, their pasts and their personalities rewritten on a cosmic scale. To make matters worse for the League, several new foes surfaced as well.

"The Awakening is complete. The Forever Crisis will come. The beginning and the end..."

THE KINDRED

THE KINDRED

The Kindred were four massive, city-sized aliens that used people—and heroes—as power sources. They were made up of millions of possessed humans joined together and transformed into singular entities. Having manifested on Earth, they performed a ritual known as the Awakening to bring about an event they called the Forever Crisis. Though the Kindred completed the ritual, the Justice League was able to disrupt the entities and rescue the people they were composed of. However, the League was left wondering what the Forever Crisis might be.

DAVID GRAVES

An author inspired to write about the Justice League after he was saved by the newly assembled heroes, David Graves was shattered when his family died and he was diagnosed with an untreatable illness. Originally believing the Justice League to be modern incarnations of the mythical gods, Graves lost his mind as a result of his personal tragedies, for which he blamed his former idols. Disappearing for years, he returned brandishing mystical powers and determined to tear the League apart through their public liaison, Steve Trevor. Graves tortured Trevor, using him to break into the League's headquarters and almost succeeded in his deranged mission.

PERAXXUS

Peraxxus was a notorious mercenary who traveled the galaxy seeking worlds to destroy that he could then salvage for profitable scrap. He used robots called the Signal Men to monitor worlds and determine whether they were ready for harvesting. Coming into conflict with the Justice League International, the intergalactic villain was only vanquished after Batman and Rocket Red managed to reprogram the single-minded Signal Men. Though he vowed vengeance, Peraxxus was never heard from again. The Signal Men might have been controlled by Peraxxus, but the automaton's original creators were never discovered, and are presumed long dead.

GRAIL

The daughter of Darkseid, Lord of Apokolips, Grail was a rebellious child. Born at the same time as Wonder Woman, and to an Amazonian mother, Grail was prophesized to be a herald of destruction and an ally of the Anti-God, also known as Mobius, the Anti-Monitor. Once Grail was old enough, she actively sought her own destiny and duly allied herself with the Anti-Monitor. Hoping to use this being from the antimatter universe as a tool to crush her father, Grail enacted a plan that drew in the Justice League and nearly resulted in the destruction of all reality. When Grail mistakenly destroyed her own mother, she reconsidered her approach and decided to try and turn Darkseid's evil into a force for good.

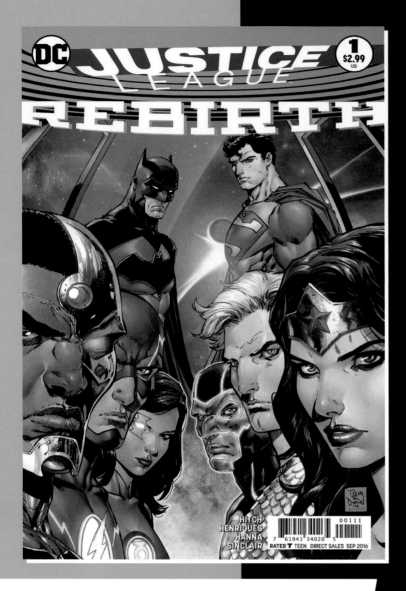

JUSTICE LEAGUE REBIRTH #1

THE SUPERMAN OF AN ALTERNATE REALITY JOINS THE JUSTICE LEAGUE.

Losing Superman has rocked the Justice League to its foundations, giving pause to even the team's most dedicated members. However, evil never rests, and it is not long before the world's greatest Super Heroes face yet another deadly alien invader—one they'll need additional help to defeat...

JULY 2016

MAIN CHARACTERS:
Superman • Batman • Wonder Woman • Aquaman • The Flash • Cyborg • Green Lantern (Jessica Cruz) • Green Lantern (Simon Baz)

SUPPORTING CHARACTERS:
Lois Lane • Jon Kent

MAIN LOCATIONS:
New York

1 While struggling to come to terms with the death of the Superman they knew, the Justice League is further disoriented by the appearance of his strange doppelgänger. During a secret meeting the team concludes they have no choice but to put their grief aside and invite the new Kryptonian into the League.

2 Elsewhere, a massive insectoid monster lands on New York. As large as Manhattan, the creature could easily crush its way across the surface of the Earth. However, instead of rampaging, the creature begins spreading spores. These smaller, marine-like creatures soar through the air and wrap themselves around the faces of any humans with whom they come into contact.

3 The new version of Superman questions his place within this alternate world, as he spends his time quietly with his family. It is his wife, former journalist Lois Lane, who convinces the hero that no matter what world he resides on, he is still Superman, and the League needs him.

4 Two Green Lanterns investigate seismic disturbances. Their investigations bring them to New York, where the Justice League has ventured inside the body of the giant extraterrestrial creature in an effort to communicate—or destroy—the invader. The alien broadcasts its intent clearly. It is merely the first of many Reapers, come to harvest humanity.

5 Realizing there can be no peace with this Reaper, the League targets the creature's brain. Joined at the last minute by Superman, the team unleashes all the power they have at their disposal on the hostile mind. Once it is disabled, they warn it to run, and to tell the universe that Earth is protected.

"It wouldn't be much of a Justice League without a Superman."

LOIS LANE KENT

6 United as a team once more—though not without reservations—the newest incarnation of the Justice League stands ready as ever to defend the world against any force that might threaten to harm humanity.

REBIRTH

After the Flashpoint event, reality was rewritten—seemingly due to the first Flash, Barry Allen's interference with the timeline. However, trapped in the interdimensional Speed Force outside of reality, his former sidekick, Wally West, saw the truth: there was another hand at work. For reasons unknown, a being beyond comprehension was manipulating all of existence.

SUFFERING SIDEKICK

In a desperate bid to reach someone, to be remembered and pulled back into existence, Wally West—now ten years younger and returned to the identity of Kid Flash—seeks out the most important people in his past. Only at the last minute is Barry Allen able to fight through his altered memories and remember his nephew, saving him from certain oblivion.

WONDERING WOMAN

With Wally's return, changes ripple through the universe. Disoriented, Wonder Woman forces herself to see the truth of her own existence with her lasso. She learns that much of what she believed is no longer reliable. Was she the illegitimate daughter of Zeus, or really sculpted from clay? Similarly, other heroes find elements of their previous lives returning, merging imperfectly with their new reality.

TWO BECOME ONE

One of the most affected heroes is Superman. After the post-Flashpoint incarnation died, the pre-Flashpoint Man of Steel returned to take his place. Now, the two Supermen merge into one being—seemingly what they were meant to be from the start. Whole again, Superman and his wife, Lois—who was similarly affected—become a full part of the new universe once more, along with their young son, Jon.

BEETLE REBORN

Blue Beetle—alias Ted Kord, who had been killed by an evil Max Lord long prior to Flashpoint—returns to existence with no awareness that he had ever died. In this new reality, Ted is now mentor to the younger magical scarab-powered Blue Beetle (Jaime Reyes), was never a member of the Justice League, and has retired from active duty as a Super Hero.

WHO WATCHES...?

Although the force behind the tampering with history remains unknown, one clue appears in Batman's cave: a smiley face button with a drop of blood on it. What purpose such an obscure and incongruous item might have, and how it could have come to exist in a place where it has no reason to be, remains a mystery...

LEAGUES OF THEIR OWN

The multiverse contains an infinite number of possible realities, with each incarnation of Earth being unique in its own way. However, on almost every world imaginable, one thing consistently holds true: somewhere, in some way, shape, or form, the Justice League can always be found.

JUSTICE ALLIANCE OF AMERICA

Although the heroes of Earth-D could not save their own version of Earth from destruction during the Crisis event, they managed to buy enough time for the people of their planet to escape to the relative safety of Earth-1. This act of heroism gave an entire parallel civilian population a second chance at existence. Regrettably, there was no way for the Justice Alliance to also save themselves.

JUST'A LOTTA ANIMALS

Entirely populated by humanoid animals, the world of Earth-C-Minus is filled with the colorful heroes of what seems like a cartoon fantasy land. Super-Squirrel, Wonder Wabbit, Batmouse, and Boyd the Robin Wonder fight villains like the Porker, Lex Lemur, and Brainy-Yak. Surviving the great Crisis event that temporarily merged all realities into one, this funhouse of a universe continues to exist—no matter how many villains attempt to erase it.

KINGDOM COME

In this parallel universe the Justice League's history is quite familiar—up to a point. Existing in an alternate future where the Joker murdered Lois Lane, this universe's Superman went into hiding. Wonder Woman has been exiled by the Amazons, while Batman operates remote vigilante drones from his underground lair. To add to this world's troubles, its superhumans are at war with one another, and humanity faces Armageddon if peace cannot be achieved.

JL-AXIS

Strongmen for the Nazi regime in an alternate universe where Hitler's forces were never defeated, these vile doppelgängers of the Justice League stand for oppression and intolerance. Fortunately, like all Nazis, their fascist regime was one that was inherently weak. The entire team of immoral superhumans was ultimately defeated by a lone warrior from another universe.

BIZARRO LEAGUE

A sub-reality created when the Joker briefly stole cosmic powers, this backward universe is inhabited by Bizarros. They used the template of Earth-1's Justice League to create their own imperfect copy of the team. Batzarro, Yellow Lantern, and Woman Wondered are just a few of the strange members of this inane parody of the League. Living on a square planet, these so-called heroes rarely escape their own world, and so they hardly encounter anyone from the rest of the universe.

THE LOVE SYNDICATE OF DREAMWORLD

Hailing from Earth-47, to escape the great Crisis these flower power heroes hid themselves within the Medusa Mask worn by the villain Psycho Pirate. Later, they grew into a fully formed parallel reality. The president of this Earth is the eternally young teenager Prez. The team is led by Sunshine Superman.

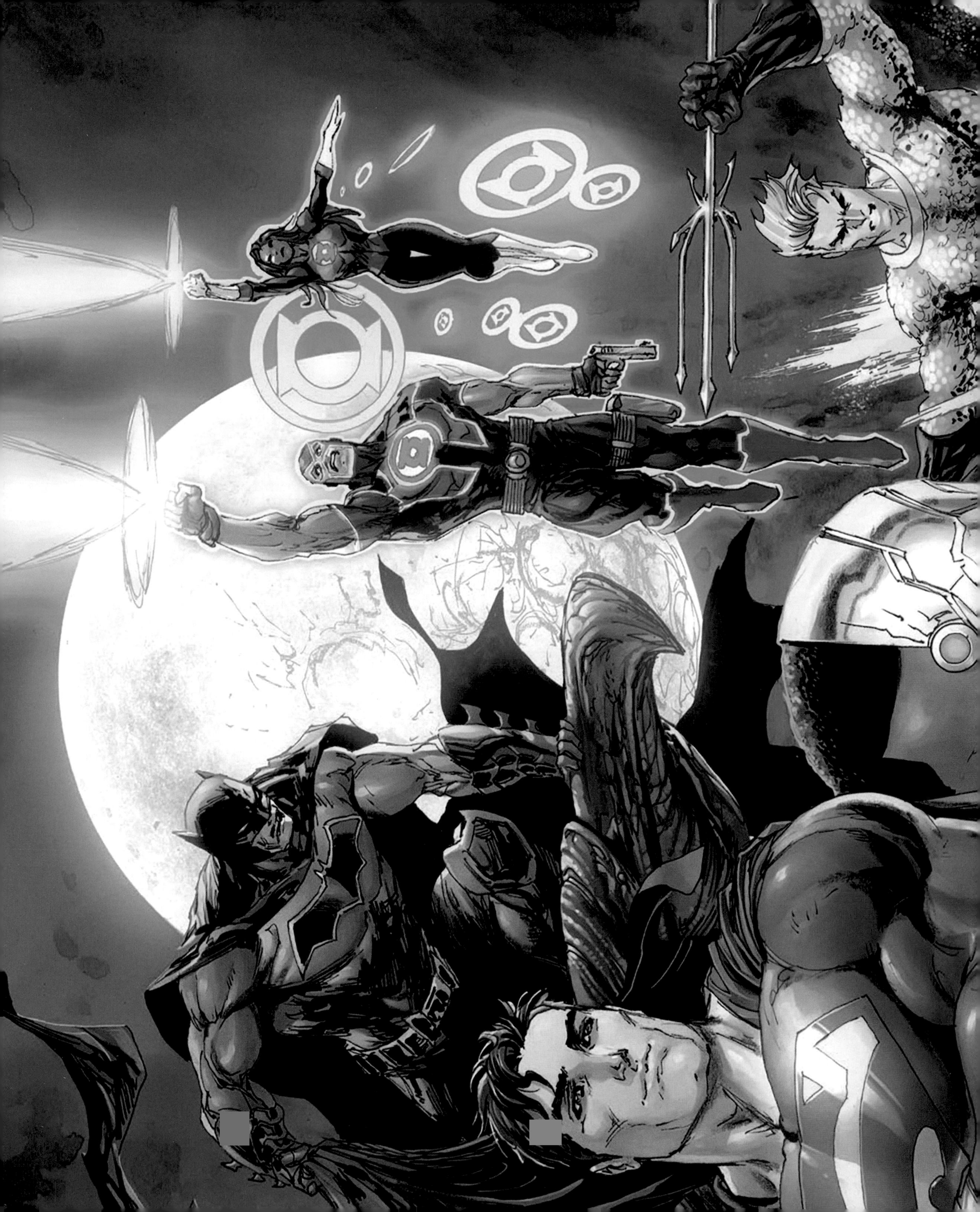

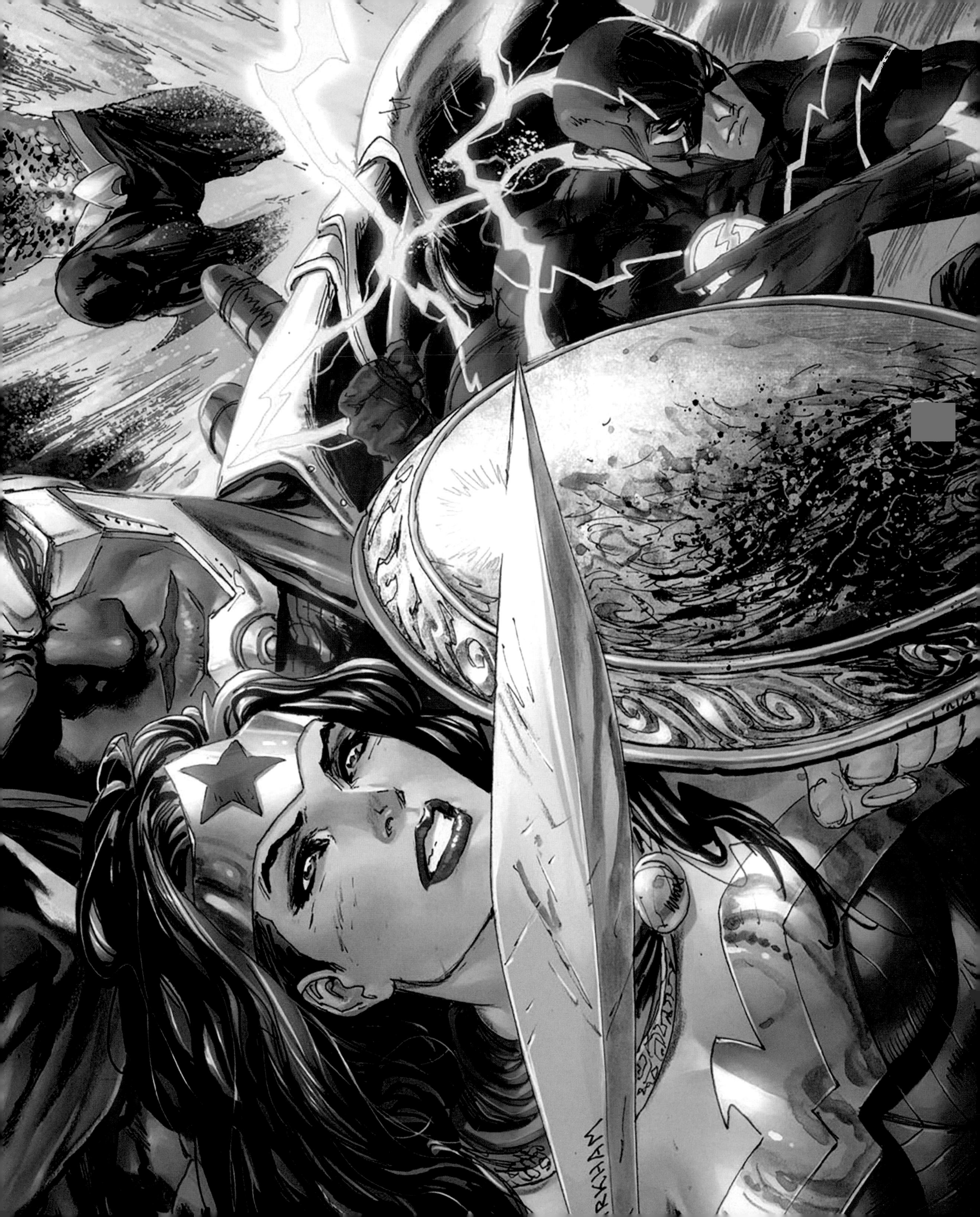

INDEX